5.1
5pts.

THEotherAMERICA

The ELDERLY

by
Gail B. Stewart

Lucent Books, P.O. Box 289011, San Diego, CA 92198-9011

These and other titles are included in *The Other America* series:

> The Homeless
> People with AIDS
> Teenage Mothers

Library of Congress Cataloging-in-Publication Data

Stewart, Gail, 1949-
    The elderly / by Gail B. Stewart
        p. cm.—(The otherAmerica)
    Includes bibliographical references (p.   ) and index.
    ISBN 1-56006-329-7 (alk. paper)
    1. Aged—United States—Interviews—Juvenile literature.
I.Title. II. Series. Stewart, Gail, 1949   Other America
HQ1064.U5S742   1996
305.26—dc20   95-40335
                                            CIP
                                          AC

The opinions of and stories told by the people in this book are entirely their own. The author has presented their accounts in their own words, and has not verified their accuracy. Thus, the author can make no claim as to the objectivity of their accounts.

Printed in the U.S.A.
Copyright © 1996 by Lucent Books, Inc.
P.O. Box 289011, San Diego, CA 92198-9011

Contents

Foreword

Perhaps more than any other nation in the world, the United States represents an ideal to many people. The ideal of equality—of opportunity, of legal rights, of protection against discrimination and oppression. To a certain extent, this image has proven accurate. But beneath this ideal lies a less idealistic fact—many segments of our society do not feel included in this vision of America.

They are the outsiders—the homeless, the elderly, people with AIDS, teenage mothers, gang members, prisoners, and countless others. When politicians and the media discuss society's ills, the members of these groups are defined as what's wrong with America; they are the people who need fixing, who need help, or increasingly, who need to take more responsibility. And as these people become society's fix-it problem, they lose all identity as individuals and become part of an anonymous group. In the media and in our minds these groups are identified by condition—a disease, crime, morality, poverty. Their condition becomes their identity, and once this occurs, in the eyes of society, they lose their humanity.

The Other America series reveals the members of these groups as individuals. Through in-depth interviews, each person tells his or her unique story. At times these stories are painful, revealing individuals who are struggling to maintain their integrity, their humanity, their lives, in the face of fear, loss, and economic and spiritual hardship. At other times, their tales are exasperating, demonstrating a litany of poor choices, shortsighted thinking, and self-gratification. Nevertheless, their identities remain distinct, their personalities diverse.

As we listen to the people of *The Other America* series describe their experiences they cease to be stereotypically defined and become tangible, individual. In the process, we may begin to understand more profoundly and think more critically about society's problems. When politicians debate, for example, whether the homeless problem is due to a poor economy or lack of initiative, it will help to read the words of the homeless. Perhaps then we can see the issue more clearly. The family who finds itself temporarily homeless because it has always been one paycheck from poverty is not the same as the mother of six who has been chronically chemically dependent. These people's circumstances are not all of one kind, and perhaps we, after all, are not so very different from them. Before we can act to solve the problems of the Other America, we must be willing to look down their path, to see their faces. And perhaps in doing so, we may find a piece of ourselves as well.

Introduction

"Just because you're sixty-five, or because you're retired, it certainly does not mean it's time to turn your toes up and die," says Martha, one of the people interviewed in this book. She is indignant at the way many people assume that to be old is to have nothing to contribute. Martha's view is shared by many older people who feel that society sees them not as individual people, but as a class of has-beens.

A VAST ARRAY OF STEREOTYPES

Being old in America is almost always a negative. As one eighty-year-old says with disgust, "It's hard to think of anything old that people really value—maybe wine, but that's it!" An old car is a junker, old clothes are frumpy and out of style. And to avoid the consequences of aging, Americans spend billions of dollars each year on hair coloring, moisturizers, plastic surgery, and other products and services to help them look less than their age.

And people who have reached the stage of old age—usually in the sixty-five-plus range—are seen by many younger people as chronically ill, lonely, fragile, and often senile. Usually, elderly people are seen as disinterested in all but their most immediate needs. In short, most of society's assumptions about old age are depressing and even somewhat frightening.

Yet a great many physicians and sociologists say that such beliefs about the elderly in American society are inaccurate. It is not true, for instance, that most old people live in nursing homes or are even chronically ill. Even though there are health problems to which older people are more susceptible—brittle bones, bad eyesight, hearing difficulty, arthritis—only about 20 percent of people over sixty-five years of age say that such problems are debilitat-

6

ing. For the vast majority of older Americans, then, old age is not a time of wheelchairs, walkers, and frequent trips to the hospital.

Nor are elderly people useless and incapable of making valuable contributions to society. Painter Henri Matisse, actors Hume Cronyn and Jessica Tandy, activist Maggie Kuhn—these are just a few of the people who have achieved fame in their elderly years. However, for all of the many famous examples of people in their seventies, eighties, or beyond who have excelled in their various fields, there are hundreds of thousands more who are not as well known. They are everyday people who find old age a time to actively pursue creative, intellectual, and physical goals. Some enter college for the first time, some write novels, some run marathons or get a black belt in karate.

NOT A HOMOGENEOUS GROUP

It is also a myth, say social scientists that the elderly are all alike. Elderly Americans today have a wide variety of cultural backgrounds. Many came to America as immigrants in the early years of this century or are children of immigrants.

Lifestyles of elderly Americans vary widely, too. In fact, according to Ken Dychtwald, author of *Age Wave: The Challenges and Opportunities of an Aging America*, one could make a case that elderly Americans are more diverse in their lifestyles than any other single age group.

"Some older people are dreadfully sick and waiting for death," he writes. "Some are physically fit and in training to run marathons. Some are abysmally poor and entirely dependent on the government for food and shelter. Others have condos in Vail and yachts in Tahiti. Some wait in breadlines for a warm meal. Others buy and sell railroads, wheat futures, and Chagalls just to keep a hand in. Some older people live rigidly conservative lifestyles, while others live extremely radical lifestyles. In many instances, older people actually live freer, more experimental lives than their children and grandchildren do."

A RELATIVELY NEW CONCERN

It is true that certain issues are more important to the elderly than to others. The cost of health care, the expense of a nursing home or in-home care, and the solvency of Social Security are all issues that the elderly worry about.

For the most part, these worries are relatively new in the history of the United States. The fact is that until this century there has not been a sizable group of older Americans. A child born in America at the time of the signing of the Declaration of Independence in 1776 had an anticipated life span of only thirty-five years. A century later, in 1876, the average American could expect to live five years beyond that.

Because of the young age at which most Americans died, few people gave serious consideration to how old age should be handled. There were no insurance benefits for the elderly, no Medicare or Social Security. To reach the age of sixty-five or beyond was a remarkable achievement, and it put one in a very select group.

But that has changed, due in large measure to the advances of science and technology. Smallpox, cholera, influenza, measles, tuberculosis—all of these have been either eliminated or controlled. No longer are they death sentences. And by eliminating the diseases that snuffed out the lives of millions of people, more Americans have been able to live longer. In 1994, in fact, a child can look forward to living to almost eighty years old. The Census Bureau predicts that by the year 2040 the life expectancy of an American will be ninety!

THE BABY BOOMERS REACHING OLD AGE

Issues of aging in America have taken on greater significance in recent years because of the aging baby boomer generation—those born between 1946 and 1964. Comprising seventy-six million people, one-third of America's population, the baby boomers have driven social trends throughout their lives.

Through studies, social scientists know that the majority of baby boomers want to deny or delay the effects of aging. They want to look and feel better and be active and useful for as long as they can. And as these seventy-six million people move toward age fifty and beyond, their voices are as loud as they always have been. Besides, simple mathematics indicates that as such a huge population ages, the unresolved political and social issues they pose will become more important.

YOICHI, MARTHA, CLARENCE, AND LOIS

The four people whose stories are contained in this book are not part of the baby boom generation. But the issues they face remain constant. To understand what some older Americans think, what they do with their time, how they look at their futures—all of these things can be instructive in understanding how people age. As Lois, one of the people interviewed in this book, remarks, "I am exactly the same person I was at fifteen, at twenty-five, at fifty. Nothing happens—zap—to you, and you're elderly. You're always you, inside."

Lois

"I'M A HOBO AT HEART. . . .
THERE ARE TOO MANY PLACES I
WANT TO SEE, TOO MANY THINGS
I WANT TO DO."

"This is Annabella Christine, the Wonderful Answering Machine," says the recorded voice on the other end of the phone. "Sometimes when you call this number, I answer. Sometimes real people do. Do you want to leave a message?"

Those who know Lois are not surprised by such a greeting. "Of course Lois would name her answering machine," laughs one friend. "I don't know anyone else who would do it, but she would. She's one of a kind. Lots of older people don't get enough calls or have enough things going on in their lives to warrant getting an answering machine. Lois's machine probably gets a good workout every day!"

"THE WAY I FEEL INSIDE IS THE WAY I'VE ALWAYS FELT"

Lois barely qualifies as an older American at just sixty-five years old. She is an attractive woman with bright blue eyes and thick white hair. "I turned white early; I think I was forty-five," she confides. "I knew it was coming, because my mother and my grandmother had really pretty white hair. I even looked forward to my hair turning, in a way! But really, forty-five was a bit young to go white, so I dyed it for a while.

"My kids said, 'Oh, Mom, don't color your hair any more—we like it white.'" Lois laughs, "Of course, that was easy for *them* to say, since it wasn't their hair! But I let it stay white—truthfully, I was getting tired of blonde hair.

"There's nothing bad about turning white; I don't feel old at all. The way I feel inside is the way I've always felt. No kidding—if you think one day you're going to wake up and say, 'I feel elderly,' think again!"

Lois has lived in the city all of her life; the home in which she grew up is only a few miles from the house in which she lives now. Even so, she is adventurous, and loves to travel. "My Dodge van is only two years old and it has ninety thousand miles on it already," she brags. "I'm a hobo at heart—just tie my red bandanna on a stick, and off I'll go. There are too many places I want to see, too many things I want to do. I love meeting new people, seeing how people live in other places."

GROWING UP IN THE DEPRESSION

Lois remembers a fairly happy childhood: "I was the oldest of three children," she says. My brother was born on my first birthday. I don't remember feeling irritated that I had to share a birthday. In fact, as we got older, I kind of saw the advantages. We'd

Lois remains an active participant in the lives of her grandchildren and enjoys being a help to them.

have birthday parties together; he'd have his friends and I'd have mine. These great, huge boy-girl parties—what a lot of fun!

"And my little brother was born when I was fifteen. By the time he came along, I was more like his mother than his sister. I did lots of babysitting, taking him with me everywhere. That's one difference between kids today and the way I grew up. An older sister was just expected to take the littlest one. Again, I don't remember resenting it, although I might have found it a bother sometimes. I do think it was kind of nice—a little like playing house except with a real baby."

Like other older Americans, Lois grew up during the Great Depression. It was a time when many people were out of work. "It

Lois is on the young side of elderly at age sixty-five, and her positive attitude and active lifestyle make her seem even younger.

was really something scary—something most people today can't even imagine," says Lois. "Banks closed, businesses failed. Everyone knew someone who had lost a job.

"We were luckier than most, though. My father was a truck driver for the city—snowplows and work vehicles and stuff like that. No matter how bad the economy was, there were still repairs to be done. Snow still had to be plowed every winter. So he worked all during the depression. We were not wealthy, but we always had food on our table—something a lot of my friends didn't have."

Her childhood was simpler than those of most children today, Lois feels. But whether that was because of the depressed economy of the 1930s or because life was just different then, she isn't sure.

"All the expensive games today—boy, I don't think even if we'd had them in the stores our parents would have bought them," she says. "We did other things for fun, and I remember them vividly! We spent lots of time at the neighborhood parks. All kids did, I think. We skated in the winter and slid down the hills. In the summer we played tag and other games—just messing around like kids do.

"Dolls were an important part of my childhood. My goodness, I must have played with dolls until I was about thirteen years old," she laughs. "I had a baby doll, but mostly I remember playing with paper dolls. We'd make them outfits—exotic clothes—any style we could dream up. It was cheap, too. And we'd collect colored bottles or cans and pretend those were the cars for the dolls to ride in. We just had to sort of create things in our minds. I wonder, do they even make paper dolls anymore?" she asks.

School Memories

For the most part, school memories are fond ones for Lois. "I was always heavy," she says, "and I was never really popular. I had friends, but wasn't one of those beautiful girls that everyone wanted to be friends with.

"I was very shy, and I remember that it really bothered me when some of the louder kids would misbehave. There was an incident that happened in Sunday school that bothered me—so much that it was years before I went back to that church!

"The teacher was really young, just a few years older than we high school kids were. The boys were very disrespectful of her, laughing at things that they shouldn't have been laughing at. That young woman was humiliated, and all I could do was to sit and feel terrible. My stomach hurt, and I felt bad all over. I don't know why the kids did that. I *do* know that when people my age talk about kids today, how disrespectful they are, and how in the old days kids were so different, I don't think it's totally accurate.

"Parents may be different today," says Lois with a shake of her head. "I think they let kids get away with an awful lot that ours wouldn't have. I know that if I got in trouble in school or Sunday school, I'd get in trouble twice. Boy, I'd be in big-time trouble at home. But kids I don't think are all that different now."

Was she a good student? "It's funny," she laughs. "You sometimes think back on yourself when you were young as a lot smarter than you were. *That's* something I notice as I get older. I was going to say I was a really good student and that I loved school. But I'm not sure that's really accurate.

"I loved English class because I was a good reader and I loved my teachers. I liked history for the same reasons. But the rest of it is a blur to me. I don't think I cared for science. If I did like it, you'd think I'd recall more about it, don't you think?"

A FAILED MARRIAGE

Lois's voice gets very quiet when she talks about her life after high school, especially her married life. It was not, she admits, a time that was pleasant.

"Married twice, divorced twice," she says with a sigh. "It was very hard for me. Something wonderful came of being married—six children—but the marriages didn't work.

"The first man I married was an alcoholic. He would go out drinking every Saturday night, and fall into bed with his clothes on, and go to Mass the next morning. It was a bad scene, really bad."

In addition to enduring a bad marriage, Lois was unhappy with the spiritual choices she made during that time. Her religion had always been important to her, providing a source of comfort. She had been raised in a Baptist church but had become a Catholic before getting married.

"I went through the whole thing—the religious classes, the instruction," she remembers. "I learned about the holy days, the catechism—all that stuff. But afterwards, after the classes were over, I didn't feel right. I can't really explain it; the Catholic Church and I just didn't fit.

"I thought there was something wrong with me," she admits. "I wondered why I couldn't fit in. After I started having kids, I went back and took the instruction again. I mean, after all, I had promised before we were married that I'd raise the kids Catholic. And I wanted to do it right—sending them to Catholic school, and the whole thing."

But as her marriage failed, Lois began wondering why she had to remain in her husband's church, especially since he was not taking an active role in the religious instruction of the children.

"It got to the point where I said to myself, hey, if I'm going to be doing the educating and the religious training, I might as well have the kids brought up in my own church, right? I was certain that I could get the support I needed, since my personal life was unraveling. So I took the kids and went back to my own church. My husband and I were divorced soon afterwards."

"THIS IS WHERE THE HURT STARTED"

Although changing churches was supposed to be helpful for Lois and her family, it proved to be a painful lesson, one that Lois says affected her profoundly.

"This is where the hurt started, I'm sure," she says. "I thought I'd be welcomed and supported, but it turned out that I was not. Because I was a woman in the process of getting a divorce, I was looked down on by my church—*my own church!*" she says, shaking her head in disgust.

"Divorce was not nearly as common as it is today. Family life was viewed in much different terms, especially in the church. The man was the head of the household, and the woman was subservient. What was so stupid was that here I had been in a marriage with a man who could not be the head of our family. I chose to end that marriage, and my church believed I was at fault.

"It was especially painful for me because I had been really involved in the church; I knew all of those people. I even served on the church board as a deacon. Yet there I was every Sunday, getting lectured from the pulpit by the minister that I was expected to place my wishes, my needs, second. What I wanted or needed for myself or my family was never more important than the wishes of the man I was married to. I was probably the only divorced person in that church, I guess. I'm not positive, but judging from the reaction I got, I'm very certain that I was.

Lois reflects upon her days as a divorced mother struggling to maintain her participation in church: "Because I was a woman in the process of getting a divorce, I was looked down on by my church."

"Imagine!" she snorts. "I'm sure there were lots of others in that church who had problems in their families, but I seemed to be the only one who couldn't keep her marriage going. That was my fault, according to them. It was a real bummer for me, every Sunday being pressured to accept my marriage the way it was." Lois scowls, remembering. "For what reason? For what?"

But even though she was hurt by the church's indifference to her personal life, Lois says that she continued as an active member.

"I stuck with it, although looking back, I'm not sure if I'd do it again. I stayed for my kids, because I felt that they needed something, you know? They had to have something spiritual to base their personal views on, even if it meant only that they'd reject it all later. That time was bad for me, but the church was good for them, so I'm not sorry.

"Besides," she says with a grin, "that time made me realize I was a feminist at heart. It made me feel rebellious, a little bit. I didn't use the word *feminist*—I probably didn't even know it then. But I really began thinking: hey, here I am with a lot of little kids on my skirts, raising them as well as I could on my own. And there is something really wrong in this world when women like me were getting the message that they were second best."

A ROLE MODEL

Lois says that as a girl growing up in the 1930s, role models in feminism were pretty scarce.

"I was raised in a good Swedish family where women were housekeepers and made coffee and took care of the children. They kept their mouths shut and obeyed their husbands," she says.

"There was one woman who was different," Lois remembers. "I had an aunt who never spoke about being equal or about having rights. But she lived her life that way. At least that's how I remember it. She married later in life, and since she'd always worked before her marriage, she saw nothing unusual about continuing to work when she married. She was always able to have the things she wanted, and I guess I look back on her as one of the only financially independent women I knew as a child.

"My uncle was a baker, and she worked in the bakery with him. She handled all the money and was treated in every way like a partner. I remember my dad and his brother wanted to buy a little place on a lake up north during the depression. Land was really cheap then, and the two of them thought they'd be smart to buy it when the price was so low. They went to my aunt to borrow the money."

Lois laughs out loud, remembering. "Wow! I really admired that! Here was this woman who had power. I mean, she didn't do anything bad or anything, but she could help people; she had the means. *She* made decisions, and people—even men—listened to her." But for all her financial independence, Lois says, her aunt still put herself in a number-two position with the men in her life.

"She always said it was because they did things for her, even though it was she who actually pulled them through life!" says Lois. "But she never saw it that way, and when I think about it now, I feel disappointed for her. Maybe deep down she knew she was equal and had respect and power, but she deferred to the men because it was simply the thing to do back then."

Lois leans back in her chair, sighing. "I don't know. I wish she were here now, so I could ask her. It never occurred to me to talk about stuff like that when I was growing up. But now I'm very curious."

A Second Marriage

Lois eventually got married again, to "a wonderful, loving man," as she refers to him. However, that marriage ended in divorce, for many of the same reasons as her first. She speaks of that relationship a little tearfully.

"Ray was a drinker, just like my first husband," she says quietly. "I didn't know it when I got married. I knew he drank sometimes, and we talked about it. But he assured me it would never be a problem.

"He even stopped drinking after we were married—at least he stopped drinking in front of me. I never saw him take another drink after our wedding. No one did. But we saw him drunk quite often. I can remember coming home one day and finding him lying in the driveway, with his head under the back of the car."

Lois says she was unwilling at first to admit that this marriage was not going to work. She took care of him, nurturing him almost as if he were one of her children.

"Things went on like that for a while," she says. "It's funny, looking back, that so much time was spent doing things for Ray that I probably knew deep down weren't helping. But I loved him so much, and he was a good husband, when he could be. He was in and out of treatment nine times. Each time, he'd vow that he would stay sober, but it would never work.

"Eventually I just had to say no, that's enough. I had to. He just couldn't straighten out, even after we separated. And I just kept thinking about how as long as we're married, I'm responsible for him. That was scary. So since he couldn't get sober, it made more sense for me and the kids to just go. We got a divorce."

Lois admits that it was one of the hardest things she'd ever done.

"It was difficult for all of us," she says. "The kids weren't toddlers or anything, but it made a real difference in their lives. Ray had been a wonderful man—when he could be—to all of us."

Achieving a Dream

Even though her personal life was in crisis, Lois found a great deal of satisfaction in her work. In the 1970s Lois was working in the civil service personnel department for the city, and was able to begin a lifelong dream of a college education. Lois's employer encouraged her to take college classes so that she could advance in her job, including increasing her salary and responsibilities.

"I'd wanted to go when I was a lot younger," she says. "I knew right after I got married and had a child. I felt that I'd made a mistake in not going on to college, but there wasn't much I could do about it at the time.

"So I started college at the age some women are grandmothers. I took advantage of the opportunity; I ran with it," she laughs. "I took all kinds of courses in areas that had become important to me—labor relations, personnel management, and most interesting of all, women's issues."

Lois says that her difficult marriages and the discrimination she had felt as a divorced mother made the education that much more important.

"I know that learning about what women have contributed to society, what women had suffered through the centuries—all that helped me be strong," she says. "It made me proud to be a woman, proud to be doing things for myself. At the beginning, my self-respect was pretty well gone, that's for sure. But learning that other women had felt the way I had—that was a revelation to me. It was like, hey, I wasn't out of line for thinking the way I did! I felt myself gaining that self-respect back. It's funny what education can do."

I Wanted to Use What I Learned

Besides giving her a sense of women's history, Lois says that the college education she received made her more aware of injustices on a day-to-day level, too.

"At that time, in the 1970s, there were two separate sections in the want ads in the paper," she says. "One for men, one for women. Believe me, I know! The men's pay was always more than that being offered a woman. It didn't matter if they were doing the same job. It was just assumed that if you were a man, you'd get a bigger salary. The man had a family—that was the rationale. As though a woman didn't!"

Lois says that she was sure that unions could be a factor in equalizing the pay among city employees.

"I was raised in a union family—real blue-collar workers," she says proudly. "I knew how much unions had done over the years for men workers. I knew they had the power to do the same for women, too."

She became active in her own employee union—the American Federation of State and Municipal Employees (AFSME)—and

Lois postponed her education, putting marriage and children ahead of career. But it didn't stop her from pursuing her education later: "I started college at the age some women are grandmothers."

started working for women's rights. She soon learned that she was not alone in her beliefs.

"There were some council members that believed in equal pay," she says. "I started communicating with them on a regular basis, and we got a good working relationship. I worked very hard on a committee within AFSME to bring about unity in pay, and it worked! I mean, it was a really, really big deal.

"I'm not taking credit for it—nothing like that," she says cheerfully. "But I'm proud that I did my best, and I believe I was someone who had an effect. From then on, the women in clerical jobs, like me, received the same salaries as the truck drivers for the city. It came down to the question of responsibility, whether the workers were in an office or driving. Since their level of responsibility was the same, the pay had to become equal, too."

Lois also takes pride in helping bring about gender equity in the kinds of tests the city gives prospective employees, too.

"That's been a pet peeve of mine for years," she says. "The way things are worded may seem trivial, but it's not a trivial matter. When questions on tests always use *he* or *him* when referring to a driver or a leader of some committee, it sends out a message. I think it's a foolish one. We changed the wording to be more fair. There are just as many *she's* for drivers as there are for office workers. I'm as proud of that as of the issue of pay."

A New Role

Although Lois has retired from her job with the city, she knows that she has important, and more personal, responsibilities in her life. Her six children are long since grown, but she is eager to remain a part of their lives, and a part of the lives of her grandchildren.

"I've always been a person who is close to her kids," she smiles. "I've always been delighted with them; I've loved seeing the kinds of choices they've made as they grew. I think that made the relationship between my young children and me very special.

"And when they're adults, the relationship changes, that's for sure. And at first it was hard. Ooooh!" she shudders, remembering. "It was really tough for me at first. When the first one left home, I felt like I was going to have a nervous breakdown. I couldn't stand the thought of being without her. But it taught me something. I had to learn to enjoy her on a different level. And I really, really do!"

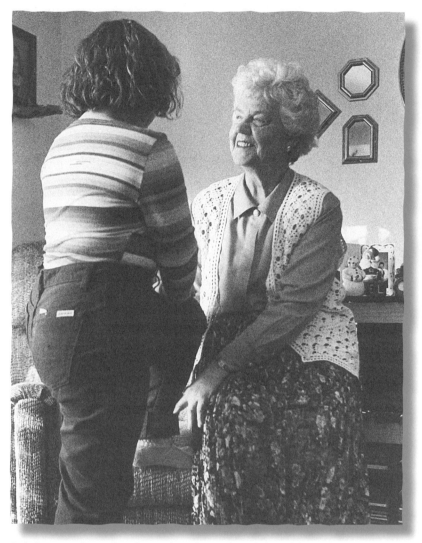

Lois is a proud grandmother and mother to her adult children: "I'm a resource person now. . . . They count on me to help when no one else can."

Today, Lois says, her children are still the most important people in her life; in fact, her best best friend in the world is her youngest daughter.

"I can talk over problems with her, or just talk about news, or things I'm excited about. I don't think I have anyone my age that I can feel so relaxed with, so able to let down my guards. I'm pretty lucky, I know that. Lots of the women I know haven't been able to make the jump from being the mother of children to the mother of adults."

"I'm a Resource Person Now"

Lois knows that even though her children are grown, she is still needed, and that makes her feel good.

"I don't need to tie their shoes or make their lunches," she laughs, "but I know they rely on me. I feel very sorry for older people who don't have the sense of being valuable or needed. That would be worse than dying, I think.

"I'm a resource person now," she explains. "They count on me to help when no one else can. They know that if I can't help, at least I'll probably be able to steer them to someone else who can. Maybe it's a question about decorating, or sewing, or fixing something around the house. I've never been an artsy-craftsy type of person, but I do know how to fix things."

She also is able to help out in more complex family matters. One of her daughters is divorced from a man who suffers from bipolar disorder, a condition that is marked by wide mood swings. He lives in a care facility and doesn't get to see his children often.

"I provide the kids with time with their father," she says simply. "I get the children—my grandchildren—and pick up their dad, and we go to a local restaurant for a meal. By the time we're through eating, he's tired out, and needs to get home. It's kind of an ordeal for someone with that disease to handle all that.

"But it's important for him to see his kids, and it's crucial for them to spend time with their dad. It just takes someone who can facilitate that. It isn't my daughter, because she just can't do it. It's hard for her. She's remarried, and it's just a strain emotionally. The things that happened between them are barriers for them. I know the problems they had weren't because he was a bad person or anything. She knows that, too, but it's hard for her to keep all the hurt and anger from their marriage out of things now. That's where I come in. I can just be a go-between and be a resource in that way."

I'm Not Afraid of Kids

Besides being close to her children, Lois has maintained close relationships with her grandchildren. Lots of older people are intimidated by children and teens, she says, but not her.

"I've got my oldest grandson living with me now," she says, pointing to a back room of her house. "He and his parents used to live right here in the city, not far from me. But they moved to the suburbs, and my grandson has a job here. I told him he could live here with me, but he had to obey the rules."

Lois says that the two of them get along fine.

"He knows I love him a lot, and I tell him I love having him here with me. He isn't here every minute," she says. "But he seems to feel comfortable enough about me to bring his friends around for a meal occasionally. They were here for Christmas dinner, in fact."

Although Lois concedes that living with a grandmother has its drawbacks for a teenage boy, the two of them have a nice relationship.

"He spends a lot of time at his friends' houses, so I suppose I cramp his style a bit," she laughs. "They smoke, and I won't allow that in my house. I'm tough; he knows there are certain rules he has to follow, and certain responsibilities, or our arrangement won't work the way it's supposed to. But we do get along, and I'm grateful for that. I enjoy listening to young people talk, enjoy hearing what they have to say about things. I'm certainly not afraid of them!

Lois takes an active part in her grandchildren's lives. "I love it when any of the grandkids call me."

"I love it when any of the grandkids call me. I don't mind that they're calling to ask a favor. Heck, that makes me feel wonderful to be asked!" she smiles. "My grandson Scott called me this morning and said, 'Grandma, can you come over and see us this afternoon, and then give Louie a ride home?' Louie is a friend from his old neighborhood and has no way to get home. I told him, 'Sure, I'd be glad to see Louie again.'

"And last winter, when wrecking crews were going to implode an old ice arena building nearby, he called and asked if I could take him over there to get pictures of it. His teacher had given him time off from class to photograph the thing coming down. I'm *glad* to be asked for favors!"

Lois says that her grandchildren are good to see in groups, but it is the individual contact that she enjoys most of all.

"I have a tradition that I take my grandchildren to Disney World as soon as they turn nine," she says. I'm lucky to have enough money saved to do that, and believe me, the kids love it. They've all gone with me, and now little Molly is the only one who is still waiting to go. Just the other day we were together and she was figuring out how much longer until she turns nine."

"I Get So Mad"

But as easygoing as she tries to be, Lois says, there are plenty of things that make her mad.

"I hate the way a lot of people drive," she says, shaking her head in disgust. "They take both lanes or stay in the left lane and go too slowly, and you can't get by them. It sounds like a little thing, but when you do as much driving as I do, it becomes a big deal."

She also dislikes the way many young people are being raised today. She knows it sounds stereotypical, she laughs, because most older people claim that things were better when they were young.

"But it's true sometimes," she says. "Look at the way many parents today make excuses for their kids, instead of letting those kids take the consequences of their actions."

She cites a recent newspaper article about a teenage boy at a local school who was expelled for bringing a knife to school to threaten another boy.

"I hated the way the kid's parents were making excuses," she says. "I mean, that kid was clearly violating school rules. Weapons have no business in a school, or even near a school. But those parents want the boy reinstated in school. What kind of a message does that send to him, or to other kids? It's crazy. Why are they angry at the school for expelling him? There are just times when we all have to accept what happens to us when we are to blame. Life isn't always fair, but by breaking the rules, we sure aren't helping."

The way older people are treated annoys her, too. She is particularly irritated by the idea that anyone who is elderly is not worth talking to—an idea that seems to be prevalent among many younger people.

"Old people aren't taken seriously by other people; that's true," she insists. "And I'll be the first to admit that they ask for it, some of them. Elderly people are often afraid, and because of that, they withdraw from so many things. Maybe younger people just assume all of us are like that, but we aren't. I get so mad when people just assume!

"I am *not* passive. I am aggressive about what I want, usually. And it infuriates me when I'm in a group of people and some younger person will seem to be talking to everyone but me. I don't really know if she's ignoring me, or thinking I don't know anything about what the others are talking about, but that's the impression I've had. And I've had it more than once," she says. "There's a kind of assumption that unless the conversation is about wrinkles or Social Security or funerals, older people aren't interested or informed. The ironic thing is that since I got my degree so recently—and in such up-to-date subjects—I sometimes feel like the *most* informed person in the group!"

"I PAID MY DUES"

It is too bad that Americans put so much emphasis on youth, Lois feels, for there is a lot about being old that is very good.

"Especially since I've been healthy," says Lois, "I've been having a wonderful time. I absolutely love being retired. Boy, I worked hard at my jobs, worked hard raising my children. I paid my dues—literally!" she says with a laugh.

"But now, that hard work and putting money aside comes in handy. I have the freedom, I have the time, and enough money to do some things I've always wanted to do. I think about going back to school to take a class or two; maybe I will do that. I look for-

ward to dancing in this square dancing group I belong to—that's
so much fun. And I plan on spending lots of time with my grandchildren, just doing things for fun.

"And I *really* think about traveling. That's the one thing I can't
seem to get enough of. I love going places I've read about and
learning about other kinds of people, other cultures. I want to try
everything I can, eat new kinds of food, listen to new languages.
There's so much about this world that is new to me!"

One trip she wants to take is to Denmark, for she already has a
friend there, a teenage boy who stayed with her for a year.

*Lois believes that many parents today fail to give their kids a sense of morality.
"Look at the way many parents today make excuses for their kids, instead of
letting those kids take the consequences of their actions."*

"His name is Soren," she says, "and he's a wonderful boy. He was a foreign exchange student. My grandson volunteered me one year as a host for a Danish student."

She rolls her eyes and shudders, remembering. "It was frightening at first, since I hadn't been responsible for cooking and caring for a teenager in many years. But after the nerve-racking part wore off, it was a lot of fun!"

Lois says that Soren most enjoyed driving while he lived with her, a privilege many Danish teens do not have in Denmark.

"I want to try everything I can, eat new kinds of food, listen to new languages."

"Driving is very expensive over there," she explains. "It is a very big, expensive deal to get your license—it costs over two thousand dollars. I guess they want people to really respect and value their licenses. Plus, in Denmark there are no drivers' training classes connected with the high schools. It's all very private, and very expensive.

"Anyway, I let him get his license here and taught him to drive. It was like having a chauffeur! We went out a lot, up to the north shore of Lake Superior—everywhere. I think the driving was the best gift I could have given him, and I know he was really excited about it. It will be fun to see Soren again."

I LOOK AT DEATH DIFFERENTLY

Lois says that there are many things she sees in a different way than when she was younger. She has learned to be more assertive when she needs help or advice; two difficult marriages taught her that.

"I do need support sometimes, and I'm no longer shy about asking for it," she smiles. "I've joined another church, one where women are as important as men. I volunteer there a lot—help out in the office, whatever they need me to do.

"Sometimes I come in depressed or feeling a little down; maybe I've even been crying about something. Someone might ask me what's wrong, and I can share a problem if I want to. We talk—we do that for each other—and it really helps. When I was struggling as a single mother of six children, I was part of Parents Without Partners for years. I think that taught me how important it is to talk about problems. And just because your kids grow up and leave home, that doesn't mean the end of problems."

Lois says she has fewer things to worry about than many elderly people, and for that she is very grateful. She has enough money to be comfortable, and she has been healthy.

"Even so, I still think the worst thing about being old is worrying about what *could* happen," she says. "I think about getting sick or hurt and having no one to take care of me. I think about that a lot, in fact. I try not to dwell on it, but it's a real worry. Most of the time I love being a single person.

"I don't fear dying the way I used to. When I was little, I was afraid of it, worrying not so much about my own death as that of my parents or grandparents. That's scary, thinking about being

"I do need support sometimes, and I'm no longer shy about asking for it. . . . I've joined another church, one where women are as important as men."

without the people who love you, who take care of you. Now it's not a dreadful thought. It seems like a natural end, the most natural thing in the world.

"Don't get me wrong," she laughs, "I hope I can live a good long time yet. I want to be active, like I said before—square dancing and traveling, and learning things. I want to participate. And I plan to—every single day I can."

A TRUE INSPIRATION

It is late afternoon, and Lois is chattering about an upcoming square dance. She has made a dress, and she's going to give it a quick press with the iron before dinner.

"Isn't it great?" she laughs, twirling the gold and green dress on its hanger. "I've bought gold shoes to match, and I'll be the belle of the ball!"

She pauses for a moment.

"You know, if I could give advice to old people today, I'd tell them all to enroll in a square dancing club. Or scuba diving, or something. Older people need to get out more, to see things that are different from what they are used to. If people don't see people from other cultures, other races except on television, they get narrow-minded and intolerant and afraid. They should keep a rich life.

"I find it helps to have a role model," she grins, pointing to a refrigerator magnet with Miss Piggy from the Muppets on it. "Miss Piggy is mine. I think anyone who is chubby, aggressive, and who wears yellow lipstick is worth looking up to, don't you?"

# Clarence

> "I'VE WORKED HARD ALL MY LIFE,
> TO DO THINGS, TO BE THE BEST I
> KNOW HOW. I THINK PEOPLE
> RECOGNIZE THAT. . . . MAYBE
> THERE'S RACISM COMING AT ME,
> BUT I DON'T THINK THERE'S VERY
> MUCH."

"Now let me show you something; you look here," says Clarence, walking slowly into a little room off the main living room. He seems to be fighting to catch his breath, and he uses the backs of chairs as he walks for support. Even though he seems a little frail looking, his rumbling bass voice is surprisingly strong.

"I just got out of the hospital, you know," he says. "I'm usually a lot stronger than this. Today I'm a little wobbly, I guess."

When he reaches his destination, however, all signs of wobbliness disappear. He stands at the entryway to the little room and points inside to the crowded walls.

"Did you ever see such a mess in your life?" he asks. His voice is gruff, but he cannot keep from grinning proudly.

Far from messy, scores of plaques and awards hang on the walls of his little office. There are testimonials from neighborhood and civic groups and from his church. There are awards for outstanding service and hard work from the Masons, the Urban League, even from the mayor. He stands patiently, giving his guests time to read each inscription.

"Looks like I got enough stuff up there for eight or nine men, right?" Clarence asks. "I worked hard; that's what I wanted you to see. I've done a lot for people over the years. I've earned respect, and I'm proud of that."

That said, Clarence turns and picks his way slowly back to a chair in the living room, wheezing and out of breath.

GROWING UP IN TOPEKA

The signs and symbols of respect that Clarence displays are priceless to him—as valuable as a good name and a good reputation, he says. He grew up in an age when African Americans fought almost insurmountable odds to gain any respect at all.

"I was born in 1907 in Topeka, Kansas," he says. "It was on Lincoln's birthday, too—February 12. My mother's family was originally from Virginia, and my father's family had migrated to Kansas from Mississippi right after the Civil War. I assume their people were slaves down there, but I don't know for sure. I don't have any history from back that far.

"What I do know is that my father was the oldest of eighteen children in his family, and my mother was the youngest of fifteen. Imagine that today! They had to learn to get along with lots of people, that's for sure, with all those brothers and sisters. Just think—thirty-one brothers and sisters between the two of them!"

Clarence's office is filled with plaques and awards: "I worked hard. . . . I've done a lot for people over the years."

Clarence's memories of his father are dim, for when he was four years old, his father died.

"It was a tragedy," he says. "He slipped on a patch of ice in the park and fractured his skull. He died instantly. My mother was left with six of us little kids to raise on her own then."

He points to a framed picture on a living room table—a photograph of a doe-eyed young woman in a polka-dot dress. The word *Mother* has been placed in the lower right-hand corner.

Clarence started working when he was seven: "I remember how good [I] felt, . . . bringing [my] three dollars' earnings to Mother."

"I have real vivid memories of being a young child in Topeka after our father died," Clarence says softly. "I remember we had neighborhood prayer meetings at our house every Wednesday night; Mother saw to that. We sang lots of happy songs, praising the Lord. When I look back, I see that she really depended on neighbors and friends to help her keep all of us together after my father was gone."

"WE WERE PROUD, AS THOUGH WE WERE GROWN-UP MEN"

This was in 1911, and there were no widow's benefits, no Social Security funds in those days. Clarence says that his mother took odd jobs cleaning for people but that a large part of the responsibility of earning money fell upon his brothers and him.

"When I was seven and my one brother was eight, we got a job during the summer at Skinner's Nurseries," he remembers. "We did lots of work—heavy work, hauling and lifting, and moving trees and shrubs around—for five cents an hour. We worked ten hours a day, six days a week.

"I remember how good we felt at the end of the week, each bringing our three dollars' earnings to Mother. Out of that, she'd give us each ten cents for spending money, and we thought that was really something!"

Free time was limited, but Clarence has happy memories of playing in the parks near his house.

"I played a little baseball," he says, "and I swam in the pool with my brothers. One thing I especially liked doing you might think is strange—I liked to play croquet. I was pretty good at it, too. We didn't have a set of our own, but there was one at the park that we set up. That was fun to play on a hot summer day.

"I'll tell you," says Clarence, leaning forward for emphasis. "We were the happiest kids in the world then. We were helping support our family. We were proud, as though we were grown-up men. It's a good, good feeling, I can tell you that."

SHINING SHOES

There was no fear of hard work in him, Clarence says, and by the time he was eight years old, he had a steady job, year round.

"I was hired at a neighborhood barbershop down by the train station," he says. "I was paid two dollars a week to keep the shop

In the eighth grade, when most children today are thinking of little more than school and friends, Clarence was offered a full-time job managing a shoe-shine parlor.

clean—swept out and tidy, you know. Plus, I had a shoe-shine stand, so that was more money."

Clarence shakes his head and smiles.

"Man, you talk about a little boy going two directions at once—I was busy! Every morning early, before school, I'd run over and open the shop, make sure everything was set for the barber to come in and start work. Then I'd go to school. After school, I'd run like crazy to get home and do my chores. Don't think just because I had a job I didn't have to do chores! Lots of the chores I did were helping old people in our neighborhood, running errands and stuff like that. Then I'd head back to the barbershop and start work. I must have slept like a dead man in those days!"

The most profitable days were Saturdays, he says, for it was then that the soldiers from nearby Fort Riley came into town for a good shave and haircut—and a shine.

"Those were my getaway days," he smiles. "I'd take off early from home—no need to worry about school on Saturday—so I could make money all day long. Shoe shines were ten cents, puttees were fifteen cents."

What were puttees? Clarence scowls, as if he cannot believe someone wouldn't know that.

"They're leggings," he explains. "Puttees are the high leggings soldiers wore back in World War I. They're made of leather, and because they have so much leather on them, I charged more for a shine. Fifteen cents was a bargain for the soldier, but it was good money for me."

"Hey, you know what a shine costs today?" he says with a grin. "Two fifty—that's a cheap one downtown at the hotels. Most places it's more than three bucks!"

Clarence worked hard for five years at his combination barbershop/shoe-shine stand, and the money he brought in really helped his family.

"When I graduated from eighth grade in 1921, I was offered another job," he says. "I was to manage a shoe-shine parlor. Manage it! Can you imagine a fourteen-year-old kid today getting an offer like that? It was a full-time job, paying an almost unheard-of fifteen dollars per week."

Clarence took the job, which today, he says, he regrets.

"It was the end of school for me. Sure, the money was great, and Mother really appreciated all the help I gave her. But now I look back and say, well, was it worth it for me to end my schooling at the eighth grade? It wasn't enough for me; I know that now."

MAKING HIS WAY

When he was seventeen, Clarence left Topeka. It was time, he felt, to see something of the world.

"It worried my mother," he says, "me leaving home like that, but I promised her I'd be good. I promised I'd live by the rules and the teachings I was brought up on, and I meant every word of that promise. You know, I've made some mistakes and done some things I shouldn't have in this life, but I always tried to keep my word about that. Those teachings were the most precious gift she could have given her children."

He had very little money, he remembers, but headed north to Minneapolis on the train, hobo style.

"It was cheap," he laughs. "And once I got there I spent the first two nights sleeping in boxcars, too. But something good happened the third day I was in the city.

"I was walking down East Hennepin Avenue downtown and was approached by a man who asked me if I had a job. I told him no. He offered me one—right there on the spot. He owned a barbershop and had a shine stand. He asked me if I had a place to live. I told him no again; I said that I was new in town and I didn't have anything yet. He told me that I looked like a nice kid and told me I could stay in the little room at the back of his shop if I needed to.

Clarence grins and slaps his knee.

"And to top it off, this man knew where I could get a dishwashing job, with a meal and a dollar fifty for working the noon hour. What great luck for me!"

"LIFE'S BEEN GOOD TO ME"

Clarence says that because the memories of his youth are so vivid, it is hard to believe that so much time has passed.

"I'm an old man now, and I accept that," he says, "but it's funny how things seem so clear in your mind. A life goes by fast, like the blink of an eye, it seems."

He's convinced, too, that the good luck he experienced when he first arrived in Minneapolis has followed him most of his life.

"Life's been good to me," he says. "I ended up getting a good, steady job. I worked with Greyhound, the bus company. I was with them fifty years, and they surely appreciated me. Hey, I was trying to get a leave of absence, a little time off, but they could hardly let me go. Chief loader I was, on the baggage platform. It was a supervisory position; I directed other men there."

Clarence says he's been fortunate in his personal life, too. Married three times, he and his first wife, Helen, had two children. Clarence is very proud of them, and says so openly.

"They're wonderful children," he says. "Guy is my son, lives in Memphis. He's a genius with videotape and things like that. My daughter Carolyn Frances has brought me nothing but joy and happiness. She's married to a fine man and has three children."

Clarence grunts and pulls himself to his feet.

"Look here, I'll show you something," he says, getting a battered scrapbook from a shelf in the dining room. He opens it to a newspaper article about a new church that has been dedicated in Madison, Wisconsin.

"Look here," he says. "This is the kind of daughter I have. She and her husband started that church in a house fourteen years ago. Now look what they've done. It's one of the most beautiful churches in the world—am I right?"

He pauses a moment, listening to movement upstairs.

Clarence and Little Miss sometimes mourn the way the world is today, especially the way children are raised. Clarence believes parents "are too busy with other business to raise [their] kids. And no child can raise his own self."

"Little Miss, you coming down?" he calls.

Grinning, he says confidentially, "That's my wife coming. Her name's Christine, but I call her Little Miss. She won't abide me calling her anything else. Fact is, if I called her Christine, I better not be within striking distance!"

"WE'RE BOTH IN BAD SHAPE"

Little Miss is in poor health, says Clarence, worse in some ways than he is. She uses a cane to get around but rarely leaves the house.

"I do all the work around here," he says. "That's not a complaint, that's just a fact. I wash the dishes, cook, take care of things. She's just not well.

"Neither am I, you know. We're both in bad shape. Take a look at the pill bottles on the kitchen table; those are all mine, that's a fact. There's pills for kidneys, pills for my blood pressure. There's pills to slow down my heartbeat, there's something there from the dermatologist for a skin condition on my leg. I got more pills than a man should see in a lifetime, that's a fact."

Little Miss, an attractive woman with a shy smile, waves from the bottom of the stairway before going into the kitchen.

"Why don't you open that door a little, Clarence?" she calls. "It's so hot in here. Aren't you hot, sitting in there with the heat on so high?"

Clarence shakes his head in mock disgust.

"That woman would like it if it felt like Alaska in here," he says with a grin. "She's trying to freeze me out of here. She's a good woman, though. Life's been very good to me."

"IT'S JUST HOW I AM"

Even though he has been plagued by some health problems, Clarence says, he has tried to be active.

"It's only been the last year or so that I've felt poorly," he explains. "I've been able to do lots of things—too many, if you want to know the truth. But it's just how I am. It's hard to say no to people. I've been active in the Elks, the Masons, the Shriners—you name it. I got hoodwinked into accepting a part-time position with the Urban League, as an outreach referral person."

Clarence says that much of his time lately has been spent working for his church, and that has been rewarding.

In spite of poor health, Clarence remains active in his church as an outreach person. "I visit all the folks who are old or sick and can't come to services."

"Sure, I've been in the choir. I'm not much good in music, but they like my deep voice. And I'm a past trustee of the church, past president of the Brotherhood Usher Board, things like that.

"But the thing that's the best is that I've been sort of the unofficial contact for shut-ins at church. I visit all the folks who are old or sick and can't come to services. I visit the nursing homes."

Clarence shakes his head sadly.

"I can't do it so much anymore, though, because I've been sick—in the hospital myself. But I don't stop. I do it by phone now; I'm on the phone all the time. People know it's me, soon as they hear my voice. It brightens their day, having someone call on them. Maybe I should have been a preacher. Man, my phone's busy all the time."

"WE TAUGHT THEM MANNERS"

Ask Clarence his views on the world today, and his cheerful outlook turns stormy.

41

"I'll tell you, there's trouble in the world, there's trouble in this life," he says mournfully. "I'll tell you something, like I'd tell anybody in the world. I raised children. Do you think that if some boy honked his horn, my daughter would race out to the street and drive away with him?"

He shakes his head in disgust.

"My daughter would have known better. When she was a teenaged girl, she wouldn't have needed me to tell her the right way. I mean it. She figured it out because of the way she was raised. She'd say to that boy, 'You don't come in and meet my daddy, I won't go with you.' That's right, that's what she'd say."

Clarence doesn't blame children for their bad manners and bad decisons as much as he blames their parents. It was different, he says, when he was a child.

"Listen to me," he says, leaning forward in his chair again. "It's the parents to blame for kids' going wild. If a child walked in here, into my home—my child—and had a handful of money, I know he didn't earn that money, he'd have to give me an accounting of it. 'Where did you get that money?' I'd ask him. I'd want to know.

"There's way too much money for kids to spend, and they act like it's nothing. Man, these shoes kids get cost more than a house! I remember going shopping with my mother and brothers before school would start in the fall. I remember the prices, too, just like it was yesterday: a pair of Boy Scout shoes for two and a quarter; a pair of corduroy breeches [pants] for two dollars; a shirt for a dollar fifty; and a three-fifty jacket."

Clarence laughs, "And we were so excited, too. I mean, we couldn't wait to start school, just to get into those new clothes!"

Today, he says, parents are simply not making the effort needed to raise their children.

"They are too busy with other business to raise those kids," he says. "And no child can raise his own self. That's crazy to think so. They need guidance, same as we did when we were little. They need to be shown how to live, the upright way."

"I USED TO SAY THIS TWENTY YEARS AGO"

But there is another reason, he says, why child rearing is more difficult than when he was a boy. Clarence's face becomes fierce in its seriousness.

The worst problem today, Clarence believes, is drugs. "That dope is the ruination of everything."

"I'll tell you something. I used to say this twenty years ago, so it isn't a new thought for me. No foreign country will ever have to use guns or missiles or anything like that to conquer America. All they have to do is keep sending that dope over here, those drugs.

"Those culprits come to school, and they introduce that dope into those young kids, so they don't know what they're doing. Too young to know better, that's right. It tears their brains apart, that stuff. Then, shooting and killing, all kinds of things happen. Here are the people in these foreign countries, they don't have enough

43

money to live on, their kids are starving. And what do they do? They keep sending those drugs over here."

Clarence is furious, and his hands are trembling as he gestures.

"All this madness, and there's no good reason for it. Where's the sense in that, I'd like someone to explain to me. That dope is the ruination of everything, and that's a fact.

"And don't tell me it's because parents are working. My mother raised us kids, all of us, on her own after my daddy died. You know what we had? Prayer. The power of prayer is a powerful thing, that's right. Teaching your child to get on the right track, that's the only thing that will save them from all that madness."

Clarence attributes his strong religious beliefs with keeping him "on the right track."

THE IMPORTANCE OF DINNER

Little Miss has come into the room and sits down heavily on a dining room chair. Her leg is very sore, she says.

"I heard you talking about all that," she says. "And Clarence, you know that it isn't only dope that's the problem. It's that drinking, too, and going to the casinos."

Clarence agrees.

"That's right," he says. "These parents gamble, and they are already poor. They're gambling away money they don't have in the lottery and everything else. They that can least afford it are throwing it away."

Clarence believes that parents waste money on fast food, and he feels that it's not only the children's nutrition that suffers for it.

"Lots of families, they don't even know how to cook anymore," he complains. "These parents take their kids out to these hamburger places—cash their check and get all that junk food. And it's expensive—hey, you could buy lots of beans and greens and good food that could feed them for a whole lot more meals.

"They could be getting a good diet and could be sitting around together at the table, like we used to. Children talk, parents talk. It's important, and nothing in this world can convince me that it isn't. It takes a little more time to raise kids like that, but it's worth it."

YOU BET I'M AFRAID

Clarence says that the decline of the family has made him afraid for the next generation.

"You hear such terrible things, such terrible things," he says. "A mother scalding her baby in hot water, a mother getting shot on her way to buy ice cream for her little girls. It makes me so sad, I feel like crying. It haunts you at night, that's what it does."

His voice takes on the rise and fall of a preacher's.

"Oh, I'll tell you, it's a vicious world we live in, a vicious world. Kids walk up and down the street, they all have guns. This neighborhood is no different. They'd shoot at you for a nickel. You can't control those guns, can't control the viciousness."

Clarence admits that he is afraid of crime, even though he doesn't get out as often as he did when he was healthy.

"There's nothing you can really do," he says. "It's being in the wrong place at the wrong time, like that. But I'll tell you, I don't want to be around any crime, anywhere—even the ones where no one is shooting guns."

He says that several years ago he went to the drugstore with a friend. To Clarence's astonishment, his friend stole some items from the store.

"I couldn't believe it," he says. "We came out of there, and he had stuff under his coat. He was a friend of mine, an old man, but he did this. I don't remember what all he took, but you can be sure he stole it. I told him, 'As long as I live, I don't ever want to go into a store with you.'

"That fellow is in the nursing home now," says Clarence. "I'll tell you, I was so frightened I didn't know what to do. You'd think the guy would have had more sense, wouldn't you? He made me like an accomplice—if you hang around with thieves, that makes you one, too, doesn't it?"

Little Miss listens quietly to Clarence, who is agitated. She changes the subject a little, saying that she is bothered by the way people seem so alone in neighborhoods these days.

"I don't know our neighbors," she says. "I know we have new ones on the one side. It's hard to meet people when you don't go out much. I just know what I see out the window.

"But there was a fire in the next block last week, in the apartments there. People went in afterwards and were taking things. Looting, taking things from their own neighbor's home. Why should they do that?"

She shakes her head and looks worried.

"It's the way of the world, I guess. Just the way of the world."

A PERSON FIRST

Clarence says that in many ways his life has been different from other African-American men, although he is powerless to explain why.

"I know *how* I'm different," he says. "But *why*? You tell me. But for all my life, I've been treated with respect—by everybody. I've always tried to be a person, not worrying about color, not worrying about how people look at my income or any of that. Everybody that knows me treats me with respect."

Could it be the white hair, the impeccably tailored suits that give him a look of dignity? Could that be why he gets so much respect?

Clarence looks pained.

"I'm trying to tell you, it's been that way all my life. Not just now. Every place I go, people come up to me, pat me on the back, greet me. People I don't even know—white, black, you name it. I've thought about it, but I don't know what it is."

Little Miss says, "Maybe you just look like you know something, Clarence. Maybe you just look approachable, you know?"

Clarence shakes his head, still pondering his own question.

"I think it has something to do with being a person, that's what I think," he finally says. "I've worked hard all my life, to do things, to be the best I know how to be. I think people recognize that, that's what I think. Maybe there's some racism coming at me, but I don't think there's very much."

"IT'S A WHITE MAN'S WORLD"

Even though he admits that his experiences with racism have been minimal, Clarence knows that he is the exception. Racism, he says, is still alive, no matter how enlightened we think our country is becoming.

"You know, the school I went to was all black until the sixth grade," Clarence says. "That's the way it was. No mixing until after sixth grade, and then we could go to the rich schools. Then they were mixed, black and white. That sounds really strange now, and people say, but look how far we've come."

He shakes his head again.

"We haven't come that far, I'll tell you that. Just look at the television every time there's a crime. You know when a white man did it, because there's no picture. But if a black man's the one who did it, you can bet there's a picture there, plain as anything.

"It's infuriating to me, I wish someone would get to those television news people. I'm a Christian man, and I try to do right, but I'll tell you, it's hard to take. I get real mad, real mad."

Clarence says that partially because of unfair or biased reporting in the news, black people, especially black men, are seen as dangerous.

"You know," he says, "we were brought over here in bondage, in slavery and in fear. If you look at the history books, the textbooks in the schools, you don't find much about Africa, nothing about our history. But there was some elegant history, some amazing accomplishments the Africans had done long ago. How

"My name, my self-respect is the most important thing I've got in this world."

come we don't hear about it? How come black children in schools
have no idea about their heritage except that they were descended
from slaves? Is that it?"

Clarence snorts.

"That's wrong. Hell, no wonder people say it's a white man's
world. Black people have had to fight hard for everything they've
gotten in this country, and they have to watch out, because there's
always someone looking to boot them in the butt even today.

"I look at Martin Luther King. How that white man could shoot
him and destroy that dream, oh, I'll tell you. I say, the black man
is a noble person in this world. He's done so much just to be
treated like a human being. Someone once said to me that it's a
miracle that black people are as nice as they are, and that's right.
That's right."

Little Miss nods her support.

"It's just instilled in people now, that racism," she says. "As
long as there are different kinds of people, black men aren't going
to be worth anything. I'm pessimistic, I am."

BASIC CONCERNS

These kinds of issues interest him, Clarence says, and he spends a lot of time thinking about them.

"I like to think over problems, things that happen in the world," Clarence says. "Sometimes they're big things, other times just ideas. I don't know what it is, but ideas come to me. I'm lying in bed and I think of something. I have a pad of paper and a pencil right next to me, right on the table by the bed, so I write things down when I think of them. Sometimes even in my sleep I think of things. Isn't that something?"

But for much of his day, he concerns himself with more basic problems and irritations.

"I hate it when people call during my dinner, trying to sell me things," he complains. "I really hate being interrupted like that. And another thing I hate is trying to make a VCR work. I don't know why they have to be so difficult. If they know that it's regular people that use the things, why do they make it so complicated?"

Clarence leans back in his chair and closes his eyes wearily. He has had a long day and he's tired. But, he says, he wants to make sure people understand one thing about him.

"My name, my self-respect is the most important thing I've got in this world," he says solemnly. "I haven't made as much money as some, but the important thing is what I did with the money I did make. You know? Lots of people make money, but they get all through and they haven't got a damned thing."

He takes out his wallet and spreads the cards from it on the table in front of him.

"I got credit cards, look. And a voting registration card, cards from the Shriners and Greyhound talking about all my years of service, of membership, I should say so. Hey, you don't get cards like these without making yourself a respected person. These are credentials that mean I have done it. No question about it, that's right."

Martha

> "FOR MANY YOUNGSTERS, THE
> TEACHER IS THE ONE AND ONLY
> PERSON WHOM THEY CAN COUNT
> ON TO BE FAIR, TO GIVE THEM
> SUPPORT."

The fifth floor of the nursing home is bright and smartly deco-
rated. There is fresh paint on the walls, and the carpeting is thick.
Colorful prints hang on the walls. There is a faint smell of antisep-
tic in the air.

An aide in a blue coat is vacuuming the dining area, and two
residents in wheelchairs are watching him. The nurses' station is
busy; buzzers sound to let attendants know where they are
needed. From down one corridor comes the sound of what at first
seems to be a young child but is identified by Martha as one of the
other residents.

"She's maybe in some pain, but I think mostly she's just not in
her right mind," Martha explains. "Every once in a while she just
starts her screaming and keeps it up twenty minutes or so. I don't
really know what her trouble is. That's just what I've overheard
some of the staff people saying, you know."

"THOSE WORDS JUST TRIP RIGHT OFF HER TONGUE"

Martha is a resident herself, although she seems to know more
about the inner workings of the nursing home than do many of
the employees. At eighty-five years old, she is lively and alert, although she spends most of her days in a wheelchair. Her face is
lined, and the shock of gray hair on her head is a bit disheveled.

"I am a solid mind trapped within a failing body," she says with a laugh.

Even though her health is marginal and she can no longer live on her own, Martha has the respect of many of the nurses on her floor.

"She's a bright woman," one of the fifth-floor nurses remarks. "That isn't unusual, for many elderly people are bright, of course. But Martha is different. She loves to talk, and I love to listen. Any topic seems to lead to a story, and she's had a very interesting life."

Another nurse agrees. "Martha has a gift for stringing words together, I'll say that. She's probably the only person in the place to use words like *reciprocity* on an everyday basis. Those words just trip right off her tongue!"

Confined to a nursing home, Martha spends most of her days in a wheelchair. "I am a solid mind trapped within a failing body."

Martha seems pleased that she has a reputation for being bright.

"I should think I'd have brains," she says with a big smile. "I was a teacher for thirty-five years. In fact, I just figured it out here a few minutes ago: between my husband, Harold, and me, we taught a total of seventy-four years. It would be a sad thing for the schoolchildren if their teachers weren't somewhat smarter than they were."

GROWING UP IN CHICAGO

Martha spent the first ten years of her life in Chicago. Her parents were both from Finland, and Finnish was the language she spoke at home. English, she says, was learned on the sidewalks in front of their Chicago apartment building.

Her father worked for the Pullman Company, which built special sleeping cars for trains. He died when Martha was only five, but she has vivid, happy memories of him.

"I can remember being a little put out when my cousin had a little doll buggy, and I didn't own one," she says. "My father and I

Martha takes an active role in the nursing home in which she lives, including reaching out to the other patients.

went shopping together. I was four years old. We took the streetcar downtown, and he bought me the most beautiful doll buggy, and a doll to go with it!"

Although this happened more than eighty years ago, Martha's voice is as excited as though it just happened.

"I remember riding that streetcar home, and it started to rain. Oh, but that rain was heavy. I sat on the seat next to my father, worrying that the buggy would be ruined once we had to get off the streetcar and walk! As it turned out, everything was fine. We had only a half block to walk from the corner to our apartment, so we got the buggy and doll home without mishap. I was so proud—two lovely gifts in one day!

"I remember another present, too. It sounds like all my father did was buy me gifts," she says with a laugh, "and that certainly isn't so. But there was an afternoon when he came home with the most beautiful pair of shoes, so soft they were more like slippers.

"They may sound very old-fashioned, compared to shoes little girls get today. They were high, soft patent leather, with six straps. The straps were fastened with pearl buttons, and there was a red tassel on each shoe! My father lifted me right up on top of our icebox and put them on for me. It's funny how certain images stay with you; I can remember looking down on my father's head while he did up those pearl buttons. I was in seventh heaven!"

School During World War I

School evokes many memories for Martha, especially her early years in Chicago schools. She was a good student, she says proudly, and known to be quite dependable.

"In third grade Mrs. Swanson chose me of all the girls to go down into the home economics room and clean up after the teachers had eaten their lunch," she says. "I took my job very seriously. Once I cut my finger on a sharp bread knife, and I thought, what do I do, what do I do."

Martha pauses in the story and purses her lips, as though she is still pondering the dilemma.

"I found a dishcloth and held my bloody finger under the water and wrapped it in the cloth. I left the bloody dishcloth there; I didn't know enough to soak it in cold water to get the stains out. Mrs. Swanson never said a thing about it, although I'm certain she knew it was me that made the mess. Even with that blemish on

As a youngster herself, Martha took charge of a younger cousin. "I was responsible because our situation forced me to be; that was all there was to it. That's how things were for us."

my record, she let me continue cleaning up that room for the teachers."

Martha remembers how the roof of her Chicago school was used for children with cases of tuberculosis, a grave health hazard in the early 1900s.

"It was like a separate school up on the roof," she says. "They called it the Fresh Air Division. I assume the authorities figured that the air up there was healthier for those children to breathe. The only enclosure or protection they had up there was a canvas tentlike thing. "It's certainly hard to imagine Chicago's air being fresh, but back then the city was not so heavily industrial as it is today. Anyway, the children who attended the Fresh Air Division arrived after the rest of us got settled and left school after we had already gone—perhaps for the fear of spreading the disease, I don't know."

Teachers had far more power in those days, she says, and some of them misused it. In fourth grade, for instance, her teacher informed the class that the world was going to end at exactly noon that day.

"I think it had something to do with the war. I'm not sure," Martha says. "But I do remember all of us sitting at our desks at noon, ready to go. Ready to go!" she wails, rolling her eyes in dismay. "Can you imagine parents today if a teacher pulled something like that—all the furor it would cause? My goodness!"

She pauses a moment to reflect.

"Of course, today everyone would know better. There is television, and everyone has access to up-to-the-minute news. But we believed that teacher; we believed it was time to go. And we were ready to go without a whimper, I guess."

"THAT'S HOW THINGS WERE"

After her father died, Martha's aunt and cousin moved into the apartment with Martha and her mother. Even though she was still a little girl, Martha found that her responsibilities increased considerably.

"One of my jobs was to take care of my cousin because his mother was a housekeeper, and very busy with her job. That little boy was quite a handful!" she says with a laugh. "I can remember helping him with his necktie, putting it on him while he lay on the floor reading comics. He was squirmy and quick when you needed him to stay still, and pokey as anything when you needed him to hurry up. Oh, some mornings I had aching in my side, worrying about being late for school because of him."

She recalls one time when she could have cheerfully killed him.

"One afternoon we were playing in the spare bedroom next to the kitchen. Our apartment was big, and my parents had designated this as my playroom," she explains. "Anyway, I got up to go into the bathroom or something, and while I was gone he dropped my doll.

"Oh, my china-headed doll, beautiful, with curly hair," Martha says mournfully. "I was so sad. But you know, I ended up feeling more sorry for my cousin than for myself. He cried and cried, completely inconsolable. Talk about criminals today that won't admit when they do something bad—he was just the opposite! I surely did feel sorry for him, but my heart was broken, too."

Martha laughs. The story, she says, had a somewhat happy ending.

"When his mother went to Finland years and years later, she brought back a replacement. It was a beautiful little doll, to take the place of the one her son had broken. She even had the name Martha stitched on her apron. And here I was a grown-up woman by then!"

Martha says that even though it was sometimes difficult and stressful caring for her young cousin, she never felt very resentful of the responsibility.

"I wasn't abandoned," she says emphatically. "I didn't complain. I was responsible because our situation forced me to be; that was all there was to it. That's how things were for us."

TO THE WOODS

Life changed dramatically at the end of fourth grade, for Martha and her mother moved to the north woods of Minnesota.

"It was so unexpected," Martha says. "I mean, we were living in Chicago, in a very busy, bustling city. And in the blink of an eye, it seemed that we were getting settled in the most rural, the wildest setting imaginable.

"My mother and my two aunts bought the place—a run-down, dilapidated farm—after my father died. We'd been vacationing up north, and a man who was giving us a ride in the lumber wagon offhandedly said, 'That place is for sale; you ladies should buy it.'

"Well, they went back to Chicago and had a conference, pooled their money, and actually bought the place! Lots and lots of land. I can't even recall how many acres, but it was two big parcels of land. All for sixteen hundred dollars. The plan was that my mother and I would live there the first year, and the aunts would take turns up there after that."

Martha says that although she was surprised that they were going to move to the north woods, she never doubted for a minute that her mother could make a go of it.

"My mother was a remarkable woman—very strong-willed," says Martha with more than a hint of pride in her voice. "She was raised in Finland, on a farm there. She knew how to handle herself. In her youth she carried two things when she was out tending sheep—an instrument like a zither and a sharp knife. No, I had no doubts that Mother could do just fine in the north woods.

"Of course, it would be primitive. There would be a lot of hard work. We would milk cows, churn butter, have a garden. But it would be cheaper there than living in Chicago. Remember, back in those days there was no welfare, no Social Security for widows and children. We just had to make our own way, and this must have seemed best to Mother."

Birthday Parties, Black Bears, and Runaway Pigs

Martha says that although their cabin in the woods was miles from town, there were plenty of interesting things going on around them.

"I can remember lots of things," she says with a smile. "I remember when a man in a cabin not far from ours advertised for a bride. A woman named Mary read his advertisement in a newspaper all the way over in Finland, if you can believe that! She came willingly to northern Minnesota as a mail-order bride.

"I can remember my mother telling me I could have a party for my tenth birthday. Quite an occasion! She said I could invite some children from school. Bear in mind, birthday parties were not nearly as common as they are today. I invited several of my classmates, but I was disappointed when only one girl came.

"Anyway, that little girl was named Sally, and she and I have been friends ever since. She lives in Sun City now, I think—an old lady like me, of course! She has often written me about that party, and how it was the first time she'd ever had either Jell-O or marshmallows. Now, where my mother found those things in the north woods, I'll never know."

Martha shakes her head and laughs at the thought.

"I can remember another time when a big black bear came out of the woods and began eating a softball in our yard. And another time, a little bear fell in a neighbor's well. What a commotion!

"The neighbor kept their milk in the well so it would stay cool. Not in the water, of course, but down deep where it was cool even in the hot summer months. Anyway, that little bear sensed that milk and knew enough to pull that bucket up by a rope. In the process, though, he lost his balance, and the poor thing tumbled into the well.

"The whole community was alerted," says Martha. "The operator used the telephones to call everyone. Eight short rings was the code for an alarm. Well, everyone started to hear about the big doings with the bear in the well, and we all went to see it.

"My memory isn't really clear on how the bear was rescued, but I think the men somehow slipped a harness on him. Anyway,

At ten, Martha would make day trips from her home in the north woods to the city of Duluth—"It's hard to imagine a ten-year-old today heading off for a day's excursion on her own."

he was yanked up and he took off into the woods, grateful for his life, I'm sure!"

One of the funniest sights Martha remembers was a runaway piglet that got trapped in a creek bed.

"Mother got it in her head that we would raise a pig," she laughs. "And Mother being Mother, she talked the shopkeeper into ordering one from the stockyards. It was a baby pig but amazingly fast and strong!

"The two of us walked to town to pick up the pig, and Mother insisted that she would carry the pig back home. They put it in a burlap sack, although why they didn't think to tie the sack, I'll never know. Anyway, this little pig fought my mother—fought, wiggled, kicked in that sack, until he got loose and ran away down the side of a rocky creek.

"Mother told me to run to a neighbor's house to get help while she stayed to keep an eye on the pig. I was able to find the father of one of my friends, and he scrambled down the side of the hill and into the creek. Pig secured! We managed to carry it home, but we both had a new respect for that animal's strength!"

A MORE PERMANENT HOME

As it turned out, the north woods became a more permanent home for Martha and her mother than they had anticipated. About a year after relocating to their home in the woods, her mother re-married. Her new husband was the village woodcutter, although he earned additional money by trapping in the woods.

"He had a young daughter, a year or so younger than I," says Martha. "So when Mother and I moved to his log cabin, I had a sister for the first time in my life."

Martha took on new responsibilities, she says, and found new freedoms as well.

"I was still dependable," she says with a smile, "and my stepfather counted on me for some important things. Since he spoke only Finnish, I was often his interpreter when he needed to negotiate with neighbors or buyers. He also depended on my stepsister and me to help with the crop of potatoes each year. Now *that* was painstaking work!

"We raised a good quality of potatoes, and so it was important to keep them free of those beetles that like to infest the plants. Our job—mine and my stepsister's—was to pick them off and put them into a tin can with kerosene, which killed them. There were different stages of these beetles, too, and they were especially hard to get off when they were just tiny, tiny buds—like little niblets.

"In a way, they were very interesting as bugs go," she says thoughtfully. "I don't know if I thought so then, but thinking about it, they were quite beautiful, with orange and yellow and black patterns on their backs."

FREEDOM TO READ

Although they lived in a far more wild setting in the woods, Martha says that she had opportunities there she had been denied in Chicago.

"One important thing that I could never do in Chicago was to go to the library on my own," she says, her mouth set in a grim line. "I liked to read, and I would have loved to go. I could have maybe accepted my mother being too protective of me had my little cousin not been allowed to travel to the library on his own. And just because he was a *boy!*" Martha says with distaste. "He never checked out books I liked."

Moving to the woods changed that, she says. Her mother subscribed to a magazine called *The Farmer's Wife*, which Martha read from cover to cover. There were Finnish newspapers, too, as well as books from the little school nearby. But best of all, says Martha, were the books she bought herself.

"I was allowed to travel all by myself to Duluth on the train," Martha says. "It's hard to imagine a ten-year-old today heading off for a day's excursion on her own, but my mother and stepfather trusted me.

"Besides," she says with pride, "I was doing work for my stepfather. He sometimes loaded a bunch of pelts in a suitcase for me to take to a buyer in the city. I'd get the check and take it home to him. One time I got a check for eight hundred dollars. And that trip I stayed overnight in a boardinghouse! Isn't that something?"

No trip to the city was complete without a visit to the Salvation Army store, where she would buy books to take home.

"I bought *Little Women, Little Men, Jo's Boys*—I loved Louisa May Alcott's books," she says. "And a lovely book of fairy tales. They were secondhand books, of course, but they were just fine for me. And the price was certainly right!"

Not for Girls

Her growing-up years were eventful and busy, says Martha, but when high school was over, she was anxious to go on with her studies. She did so, but over the loud protests of her stepfather.

"He did not feel too kindly about a girl getting an education," says Martha. "How did I get the sense of that? Well, he outright said so! My mother was determined, though, so off I went to college."

Martha studied hard to earn her teaching degree. She also met her future husband, Harold, at college. Like her, he was studying to become a teacher.

"He was a tall, good-looking man," she says with a broad smile. "My first impression was oh, my, he's tall, slender, blond, and blue-eyed, very intelligent, and a very hard worker. He was a little older than I; he'd been out of school three years, working at a boat works, saving money for school.

"We met at a college forum at the Presbyterian church near the school. It was like a get-together spot for college kids, a place to meet and talk. Well, we were both there on a Sunday afternoon, and we met like something out of a novel.

"This was in the days when young women wore hats and gloves for an afternoon outing. I stood up, and my gloves fell on the floor. Harold bent down to retrieve them. That's the kind of young man he was—very polite. He asked if he could walk me home and I said yes!"

She counts silently on her long fingers.

"Nine years—we courted nine years. He proposed the first year, of course, but I could not accept. I asked him, 'What would we live on?' Remember, this was the depression, and neither of us had any money. I was just eighteen."

Martha says wistfully, "In a way, it would have been nice if we'd married earlier. As it was, we were married forty-six years. I wanted to get to fifty, but we didn't make it. Harold died of cancer back in 1986 and had felt poorly for some time. Anyway, that long courtship was just *too* long, I suppose. But we had many wonderful years, and I wouldn't trade them at all."

They lived most of their lives in Minnesota, except for an eight-year stint in Onekama, Michigan. Martha says that Onekama brings back a flood of happy memories.

"It was the most beautiful lake town," she says. "Today it's different, I was there not long ago. It's all built up and crowded. But then it was lovely. My husband taught science there for a time and then was elected superintendent of schools. And my daughter was born there, so my memories are *very* pleasant!"

Martha taught in Michigan, too, as did a surprising number of Onekama residents.

"These were the war years—World War II," she explains. "I had a teaching certificate for elementary, but they needed people to teach high school kids. So I did—mathematics and literature. And home economics, too. I think every matron who had ever stepped inside a classroom in those days was asked to teach home economics! There was a shortage of teachers in those emergency times, and we all had to do our part."

FIRST AND FOREMOST

Being a teacher was more rewarding than anything she could have done, says Martha, and she would like nothing better than being remembered as a good teacher.

"I loved it," she says modestly, "and for that reason I know I was good at it. I don't think a person could love their job so much and do it poorly, do you? I couldn't help but be good!"

Martha explains that she was a loving teacher who tried to be accessible to her students, but she was firm, too.

"I allowed no hanky-panky," she says, waggling a finger. "I expected my pupils to do their best, and we structured our learning that way. There was such a lot of work for them to do, so many wonderful things to learn. But there are just as many wonderful ways to approach learning. That I know for certain.

"Besides," she says with a grin, "I think the school appreciated me. I retired on a Thursday, you know, and by the following Tuesday I was asked to come back and help break in some new teachers. They must have thought I had been doing something right!"

"LIKE THEY WERE VIEWING A BODY IN A MORGUE"

"I'll tell you one time that I really treasure—a very good memory of the relationship between me and my students," she says. "I was going to have a birthday. I forget how old I was. Around fifty, I think.

"Anyway, some of the children in my sixth-grade class had found out about my coming birthday and had chipped in money for a cake. One of the children lived near a bakery, and she was commissioned by the others to bring the cake to school, so they could have a party for me."

Martha said that at the last minute, however, the principal got wind of the idea. He told her that under no circumstances was a birthday party to be permitted.

Martha looks back on her career as a teacher as being her contribution to society: "I loved it . . . and for that reason I know I was good at it. I don't think a person could love their job so much and do it poorly, do you?"

"And yet, I could see out the window as he was talking," she says. "And here came my pupils, with the big white box from the bakery. I thought to myself, what shall I do? What shall I do?

"Luckily, the principal hadn't seen the children coming with the cake! Anyway, I knew I had to think fast. I had that kind of bulletin board in my classroom that could be reversed, with a little space behind it. So when the children came in, I told them to put the cake in there for now, until we decided what to do.

"Oh, they were sad! Everyone filed by the hidden shelf for a look at the beautiful cake. They filed by it like they were viewing a body in a morgue! I felt so bad for them; their little faces looked so disappointed."

Martha says that to give up on the birthday party would have been wrong, so she found another solution.

"I said, 'Okay, kids, you know where I live. Today is Friday. You come to my house tomorrow at two o'clock.' I took the cake home with me. And the next day the kids came. Not all, of course, but a good majority of them. I had made popcorn, and we had Kool-Aid and peanuts and, of course, the cake."

The party was a huge success, she says, although by today's standards it might seem a little tame.

"We had a lovely time," Martha smiles. "We had no games or anything; we just sat around and talked. The children seemed excited to be visiting me, to be seeing me outside of school. Some had even brought gifts!"

She says that in her long life she has learned the value of taking matters into her own hands occasionally, especially when the happiness of children is concerned.

"Sometimes the powers that be don't have a clue of how to proceed," Martha says with a roll of her eyes. "I remember when the police department used to have a picnic for the children who had been school patrols each year. Well, one year the police just decided that they weren't doing it any longer. The kids were so disappointed, for many of them had heard about the picnic from older brothers and sisters who'd been patrols other years.

"Well, I thought, why can't we just organize our own, for our patrols in our school? So I did! We ordered hamburgers and fries and Cokes—that kind of thing—and made up games and even had some prizes. We certainly didn't need the police department, I guess!"

"I Doubt That I'd Care About Teaching These Days"

But for all of her fond memories of teaching, Martha says that she would be hesitant to choose teaching as a career if she were a young woman today.

"I don't think I'd know what to do in a classroom today, because of the computers," she says. "I wouldn't have any idea of how to progress. When I went back to observe a school not too long ago, I saw an entire library of computers—twenty in a room. Twenty! Just imagine, twenty places where children could learn at one time on these machines.

But more than the changing curriculum, Martha says that the attitude of children today seems different from when she taught.

"I doubt that I'd care about teaching these days," she sighs. "I am disappointed, I think, in how kids are these days. So many of them have so much at their fingertips, but they don't take advantage of it. When I hear about so many of these children from wealthy families taking drugs or committing acts of vandalism—oh! It makes me so depressed.

"The problem is, I think, that parents aren't home for their children the way they used to be. They're working, and too many center-city youngsters have the huge responsibility of taking care of their siblings. They don't feel the same sense of that responsibility, though—not like children did in the old days. They don't know how to properly guide those younger brothers or sisters because many of them haven't been properly guided themselves."

Martha says that the lack of guidance at home makes children harder to teach.

"My first job would be to build a rapport with them, to give them the idea that here is someone that knows a little more than they do. Give them the notion that it's worthwhile to come to school. Nowadays, for many youngsters, the teacher is the one and only person whom they can count on to be fair, to give them support. That's tragic. But what a large responsibility for a teacher today!"

Keeping Busy

Martha says that her life today centers on the nursing home where she lives, and although she would certainly be happier in her own home, she knows that would be impossible.

"I've had some health problems," she says. "I have had cancer surgery, and I guess I'm fine. My main problem is this condition where my legs don't work like they should. I have braces on both legs, although I'm told I should use my walker to get in and out of the dining room. It's a funny feeling in my hands and feet, as though someone were rubbing them with a dry washcloth, or as though I were touching dry tapioca—a tingling feeling."

Like many elderly people, Martha bemoans the way children are raised today. "Parents aren't home for their children the way they used to be. They're working, and too many . . . youngsters have the huge responsibility of taking care of their siblings."

Physical therapy sessions are available at her residence, she says, but they are too expensive.

"I don't go," she says. "They cost $119 per session. Can you believe that? So instead, I do exercises on my own, when I'm lying in bed. Or in the mornings, I pull the blankets off my legs and let the sun shine on my ankles. That feels good, and the price is right!"

Resigned to living at the nursing home, Martha does the best she can to make her little room seem as warm and comfortable as possible. Pictures, cards, and letters are pinned up with a school-teacher's eye for symmetry and color. She seems to have many friends who write to her.

"Oh, yes," she smiles, "I write lots of postcards and letters to friends, ex-colleagues. I have two friends who speak Finnish, and I enjoy when they call. It's a chance to use my native language and to feel young again! I also get calls from my daughter, who lives out east, in New Jersey. I have two lovely grandchildren, whom I don't get to see as often as I would like."

She points at a picture prominently displayed on her table.

"One of my grandchildren will be sixteen in two weeks," she says, "and the boy is in his second year at Yale. They're just like my daughter, very bright, very well educated. I'm quite proud of them."

GETTING USED TO BEING ELDERLY

Martha says that even though she may look her age, she does not feel much different from how she did as a girl.

"My mother used to say that you're only as old as you feel, and sometimes I feel very young," she says. "My mind is active, and I don't think I've slowed down mentally at all. I still enjoy reading and talking with friends. I even write an occasional short story. I'd like to look into having it published."

Even though she keeps busy, Martha says that group living has been a difficult adjustment.

"The food, for one thing, has been difficult," she says with a groan. "I find as I get older and older, I really yearn for the foods I grew up with. Such good home-cooked meals, and desserts like rice pudding—my absolute favorite. Whole milk, rice, and salt, in the heavy brown dish my mother used.

"No sugar," Margaret warns, waggling a finger. "It wasn't necessary. It was my most favorite thing in the world to eat. Mother would always bake it for my homecoming, when I came back from college, or for a visit to the woods after I grew up.

"Macaroni is another thing I miss," she says. "I loved it the way we used to cook it when I was a girl: baked in a wood-burning stove for a long time. We had no hard cheese to use—a little curds and whey, maybe, and some butter, but nothing else. Magnificent!

"I even miss the fish we used to eat. My stepfather and I would catch lots and lots of fish, especially when the sucker run was on. You could go to a creek and almost scoop them out with a barrel. They were like salmon spawning, you see. We pickled them, and they were delicious."

Besides not having many of the foods she likes, Martha says that she also misses the control she had when she lived alone.

"I'm a very social person," she says, "but I do value my privacy. When I first came here, I felt like I was being turned inside out, upside down, every which way at first. I felt as though I was being invaded constantly by the staff, although I have nothing but praise for them. I'm used to being taken to the bathroom by aides who are either male or female. But it has not been easy!"

"I write lots of postcards and letters to friends, ex-colleagues. . . . I also get calls from my daughter, who lives out east."

I Feel So Sorry for Some of Them

As uncomfortable as it has been for her, Martha acknowledges that there are others at the nursing home who are far worse off.

"I see them in the dining room," Martha says sadly. "I feel so sorry for those old people—the ones that need to be fed, the ones who don't have anything at all going on in their lives. It's hard to imagine what it would be like being in their situation.

"The idea of my dying isn't one I dwell on. I don't think too much about it, actually. I guess when my time is up, my time is up, right? I just hope I don't suffer or become like these old people, so lost."

She brightens. There is so much she can do that she should be grateful, she says.

"There are big doings here this week, you know," she says. "In honor of some of the residents, each day they are honoring a different nationality. Yesterday was Swedish day—we've got lots of those here. Swedish music, herring and crackers, the whole thing."

Martha says that she tries to take an active part in whatever is going on, and that makes life all the more interesting.

"I have sort of appointed myself resident historian," she laughs. "I have a little camera and take lots of pictures when things are happening around here. I always get double prints and hand them out to some of the residents. They get so excited; they're like little kids when they see themselves.

"I myself enjoy some of the classes," Martha explains. "I do water coloring. I took a ceramics class and made two cats with green eyes. One I gave to a friend. I was pretty proud of it. And I love to sing in the choir.

"I even got a chance to use one of those new machines—those karaoke machines," she says. "I sang 'The Yellow Rose of Texas,' I think, and it was a lot of fun. They should have those on every floor, I think. But maybe the staff would mutiny or something, I don't know."

Not Many Regrets

As she looks back on her eighty-five years, are there things Martha would have done differently, things that she regrets?

She thinks hard for almost a minute, frowning.

"I wish I'd taken voice lessons when I was young. Many of the people here think my voice is pleasant, but I would love to have

Martha plays piano, and still very much enjoys singing. "I wish I'd taken voice lessons when I was young."

had some training. And I wish my parents had been able to afford an instrument. I think the saxophone would have been my choice," she says.

"And in the last few months I have been remembering my stepfather. He has been dead for many years, but I can remember him sitting in the living room on Sundays, singing Finnish folk songs in his whiskey tenor.

"He was hardly ever home, with the farming, the trapping, and the woodcutting. But I think maybe he was lonely. I wish sometimes that I'd walked into the living room and sung with him, or at least sat with him and listened. It's funny, isn't it, the things you think when you get old?"

Yoichi

"I KNOW THERE ARE SOME
ELDERLY PEOPLE WHO DO THAT
SORT OF THING—GO TO THE
LIBRARY, OR TO SCHOOLS TO
READ TO CHILDREN. I COULD
NEVER DO THAT, I'D BE
AFRAID. . . . I DON'T KNOW HOW
OTHER PEOPLE DO THAT, JUST
WALK INTO A CLASSROOM AND
FEEL COMFORTABLE READING TO
CHILDREN."

It is an old house, one that was stately in its day. But now it seems colorless and abandoned, with curtains drawn in every window. There are no flower beds or gardens; the house is in need of paint.

Inside, the house smells old and musty. There are mountains of yellowed newspapers stacked against the walls, as well as boxes of personal papers and photographs. The edge of a wallpaper strip dangles from one wall, the glue giving way after many years.

Yoichi lives here alone. It is the house his parents bought when they moved here from Seattle fifty years ago. They have died, as has one of his sisters who lived here, too. Yoichi apologizes for the clutter.

"I am planning on moving," he explains. "I'm sorting through all this stuff, and it's hard to know what to keep and what to throw away. I do a little of it each day. Eventually, maybe, I'll get caught up."

GROWING UP IN SEATTLE

Yoichi is a handsome man who looks and acts younger than his seventy-five years. He seems both pleased and a little nervous about having a visitor—he does not get many, he says. He sits stiffly on a chair in his living room, folding his hands in his lap, then unfolding them, unsure of what to do.

"I was born in Japan," he says. "My family moved to Seattle when I was just an infant. There was a large Japanese community there—several thousand people in the 1920s, I think. The climate there was a lot like Japan, so that may be the reason so many Japanese stayed, I don't know.

"My father got work in a Japanese department store right after we arrived, but he knew he didn't want to stay there. Photogra-

Yoichi's house suffers from inadequate wiring. It is difficult, at seventy-five, to complete the major repairs around the house.

phy was his real love, and it was his goal to find work taking pictures.

"My father knew no English at all when he first arrived. But he picked it up quickly, and I admire him for that," says Yoichi proudly. "He spoke better English than most Japanese. My mother was different; she never did become very fluent in English. She knew just enough to get by and to get a job as a seamstress."

Eventually Yoichi's father did get a job with a photographer in Seattle. Instead of taking pictures, however, Yoichi's father was hired as a darkroom worker, enlarging prints to make portraits of family gatherings and weddings.

"Even though it was not what he might have intended, he enjoyed it," says Yoichi. "He was able to take the hobby he loved and make a trade of it. His English was good enough that a white photographer hired him, and that says something about his diligence, I think."

Yoichi says that his youth in Seattle was very happy. He was active both in his church and in Boy Scouts.

"I loved to be outside," remembers Yoichi with a smile. "I was in a Boy Scout troop with all Japanese boys, and we had a great leader. He was white, the minister of our church, too. What a one-of-a-kind man! He was a friend to all the boys, and you could tell by the way he was that he liked all the kids.

"He would take us on long hikes and climbs, lasting as long as five or six days! We'd go about one hundred miles out from Seattle and take the trails that circled Mount Rainier. I have done lots of camping and hiking since. That leader really gave us a gift when he taught us those things.

"Listen," Yoichi says proudly, "I climbed Mount Rainier when I was sixty-four years old—all the way to the top. And I've climbed down the walls of the Grand Canyon—all the way to the bottom."

A FORCED MOVE

Life in Seattle was uneventful, he says, until World War II began. When the Japanese bombed Pearl Harbor late in 1941, the U.S. government forced all Japanese people to move inland, away from the coast. Like all other Japanese in Seattle, Yoichi's family was relocated.

"It is one of the most vivid memories of my youth," he says. "Do you think children today even know about that? I'm not sure many of them do! The government said it was a precautionary move," he remembers, "against Japanese people committing any treasonous acts. I guess that means helping Japan during the war in its fight with the United States. People were suspected of sending radio messages to the enemy, to Japanese ships."

Yoichi said that it was a frantic time in his Seattle neighborhood when the relocation project was announced.

"The government was sending us to special internment camps. There were notices everywhere, on every telephone pole. The newspapers and radio were full of announcements, too. No one had much time to get rid of their belongings; you couldn't take much, because space was limited. And of course, no one knew how long we would be away from our homes."

"In my family, we sold most of our possessions. My father was very unhappy, and he was unsure whether we'd be coming back to Seattle at all. And since the whole project came about so quickly, we sold things at very low prices. It was sad, like a going-out-of-business sale."

Yoichi says that many Japanese who were U.S. citizens were angry about the way the government moved them. He says there was a great deal of anti-Japanese feeling in those days, even before the bombing of Pearl Harbor.

"I think like a lot of the others that were interned in camps," he says. "I remember how many nice Japanese farming communities there were before the war, and how well kept the farms were. The land was rich and fertile, and the farmers did well. I think many American Caucasians resented the Japanese people being there, having such a good life. I don't know if that's true, but I have always thought so. And when we were forced to move to the camps, the white farmers sure did not waste any time in taking over those farms!"

LIFE IN THE INTERNMENT CAMP

The Seattle families were sent to temporary camps for a few months, while they waited for the more permanent camps to be constructed.

"We had no preconceived idea of what the camps would be like," says Yoichi. "None of us in my family did, anyway. There were no houses, or anything like a single dwelling. Everyone lived in long barracks, partitioned off with curtains for individual families. One room for all of us—me, my parents, and my two sisters. My one sister was studying to be a nurse, so she would be allowed to leave after about a year.

"There was a community mess hall, where all the meals were eaten. There was a community laundry and latrines. It was very much like a military camp, for that is really what it was, you see. It was run by the army."

The permanent camp to which Yoichi's family was assigned was in southern Idaho. It was a little more substantial than the

Yoichi's family was interned at a Japanese camp during World War II. "I think many American Caucasians resented the Japanese people being there, having such a good life."

temporary camp, but Yoichi still recalls being resentful.

"It was not home. We could not help being bitter about being forced from home. We were not treated badly or anything; at least I have no memory of it. But we were prisoners in a way. We'd all had nice, normal lives back in Seattle, but we were not permitted to live in our home."

"Boy, Was It Dusty!"

Yoichi remembers that one of the most unpleasant things about the camps was the lack of cleanliness, and that bothered many of the Japanese families.

"The barracks at the Idaho camp were not neat and tidy the way we Japanese were used to keeping our homes. I remember my mother being sad about that. The exteriors were tar paper, and the floors always looked dirty, no matter how hard you swept them.

"They had dug up all the sagebrush when they built the camps, and there was nothing left to hold the dirt down. There was dirt and dust blowing everywhere—boy, was it dusty!" he laughs. "And all that dirt blowing around outside made the barracks dusty all the time, too. Our dishes were dirty; the bedding was always gritty."

Yoichi says that it was important for the Japanese to establish some kind of a normal life in very unusual circumstances—especially for the young children.

"Life went on," he says. "There were schools at the camps. I had never been a great student, but because I was skilled at mathematics, I was hired as a teacher. I had no license or anything, but our little schools couldn't be too choosy.

"The government referred to us as colonist teachers. Quite a euphemism, eh?" he smiles. "I taught children mathematics, both grade school and high school level."

It was important for everyone to have some responsibility, some function, Yoichi says, even if it was minimal.

"My father worked as an X-ray technician in the hospital. I guess that was as close to photography as he could get. My mother was a waitress, and that was great for our family, since she got to bring home all the leftovers! These jobs were pretty menial, as I look back, for the top wage at the camp was only nineteen dollars per month."

Ways Out

Although Japanese in the camps were being held against their will, Yoichi says, they were not prisoners in the strictest sense of the word. There were some legitimate ways out of the camps, such as having a definite job opportunity—as long as the job was far away from the West Coast.

"We were lucky in that way," says Yoichi. "My sister was really fortunate, because she was accepted as a student nurse in Rochester, Minnesota. I'm sure she wouldn't have been able to leave if the school had been in California or back in Seattle. But since she was inland, it was OK. She left, promising to look for a job for my father in Minnesota."

Yoichi, too, was able to leave the camp as a farmworker.

"There was a big shortage of farmworkers during the war," he explains. "Most of the young men were fighting. So, many of the young Japanese men were permitted to work in Idaho picking vegetables. I picked potatoes—so many, so many potatoes. So backbreaking! There were no machines to do this work, as there are today."

Getting On with Life

Eventually, Yoichi's father was able to secure a job as a photographer in Minnesota, so the family was allowed to move. For Yoichi that was good news: not only could he stop picking potatoes, but he could also get on with the education that had been interrupted by the move to the camp.

"I had already been to college in Seattle, but I had never finished," he says. "I got odd jobs for a while—shipping clerk, draftsman. Finally I entered the University of Minnesota in 1944. I was older than most of the students, but that was OK. I was just happy to be there. And I graduated with a degree in mathematics."

Yoichi had little trouble getting a job with his new degree.

He took a position in an engineering laboratory, working with wind tunnels.

"It was interesting to me," he explains, "working out the different drags various objects had as they traveled through air. I did that for nine years and then got another job in another laboratory, this time doing experiments for the U.S. military.

"I did research on missile guidance systems. My job was to help program the computer systems that guide the missiles, to keep

Ironically, after living in an internment camp during World War II because the Japanese were considered potential security risks, Yoichi went on to a career in developing military weapons systems for the United States.

them from veering off course. It was a big responsibility, because the computer system was the control. Any error as the missile traveled through the air had to be corrected by the computer program."

Yoichi enjoyed his work and prided himself for always being on time and missing very little time on the job.

"I was always a good worker," he says. "I caused no trouble, never asked for special favors or privileges. I tried to be friendly to my coworkers, although that part was hard for me, since I'm not too outgoing. I did enjoy the traveling part of my work. The missile I worked on was tested at Cape Canaveral in Florida and at an air force base in California. Traveling was the most fun part of my job."

"I HAD FRIENDS BACK IN THE SIXTIES"

Yoichi admits that his personal life has not been as fulfilling as his career. Single all his life, he feels that in some ways it was his Japanese heritage that was partly responsible for his solitary life.

"Japan has a different view of old people than America," Yoichi says. "The way I treated my parents, the way they expected me to be, was a Japanese way, with great respect. Is that good? In some ways, yes, of course. But in a way, the way I had to be with my parents was one of my problems.

"They expected me, as their son, to take care of them when they were old. My life became centered around them instead of on other things. I could not travel or go out as often. I was not free to move out, to move away. And at a time when others my age were getting married, I was busy at home. Things were very confining for me."

Yoichi says that he did the best he could not to be isolated from people his own age.

"I had friends back in the sixties," he says. "I went skiing on weekends during the winter, and I'd go camping or climbing. I sometimes did things with people from work. But I don't see any of those people now. They mostly have families or have moved. One has died recently; I did hear about that. I don't know—for the most part, I have not kept track of their lives."

A SOLITARY LIFE

Yoichi has been retired for about fourteen years, he says, and that has been a big change in his life. While retirement has brought about some positive changes, he says, there have been difficult ones, too.

"Work is the way I socialized with other people, but now I don't see too many people," he explains. "It used to be automatic, going into a building where other people were working. They'd talk to me, I'd talk to them. That part I miss.

"But there are benefits to being retired. I no longer have to structure my days around work. I can do what I want. I don't need to worry about looking for a job. That's harder and harder for young people nowadays, I think. So I am spared that. And because I saved my money when I worked, and because I have no wife or children to spend my money on, I have enough to be comfortable."

What does he do with his unstructured time? Yoichi sheepishly admits that he watches far too much television—a problem, he says, for many people who are alone.

"I have a TV problem," he says. "I love to have it on, and I think it's company for me. I like science programs, ones about nature or physics. I don't have cable, but I think I'd like to try it. I watch news programs, too, and baseball. I really enjoy following baseball—especially now that the strike is over!"

Most of his days are the same, he says.

"I get up around eight o'clock and putter around, just doing little things. I watch one of those early shows like *Good Morning America* or *Today*. I read the paper. I can take more than an hour doing that. A few chores, and my morning is pretty well shot.

Always shy, Yoichi's life has become more solitary since he does not have work to help him socialize.

80

"One day each week I do errands—go to the grocery store, the bank, things like that. Not very exciting," he says with a smile. "I really hate shopping. It seems like a lot of bother to me. Mostly I have no patience for the parking of the car. Usually when I have to go to a mall or shopping center, I park very far from the building, the farthest lot away. I like the exercise, and no one fights over the parking spaces!"

BEING AN OLD MAN

Yoichi says that he is very fortunate to be in fairly good health, unlike many people of his age.

"I have a minor heart problem," he shrugs, "but nothing serious. The only thing I'm not supposed to do is shovel snow, and that's all right with me! I do everything else. I rake leaves, things like that. I feel fit; I expect to be around for many years."

Besides exercising, Yoichi says that his eating habits have been good all his life, and he attributes his good health to his choice of foods.

"I like going to the Japanese grocer," he says. "That is somewhat nostalgic for me, because I am reminded of the kinds of foods my mother prepared for us a long time ago. I don't cook as many dishes as she did, but I eat a lot of salmon and rice and vegetables.

"The one American treat I became hooked on was ice cream," he laughs. "But the doctors said no more of that, so I switched to the fat-free stuff. I eat a lot of that ice cream."

Even though Yoichi is in good health, he still admits that there are aspects of being an old man that bother him.

"I know people treat the old differently than they treat the young," he says. "Especially on the road—drivers are not polite to me. I know I'm a cautious driver, maybe a little slow on the highway, but I hate it when people drive up fast behind me and make bad gestures because I don't speed up like them. It makes me mad."

Yoichi says that as an old man he tends to think about dying more than he did when he was younger.

"I don't expect to go soon," he laughs, "but it is on my mind occasionally. Well, more than occasionally. You hear on television of people dying who are your peers, your age group. And the newspaper obituaries are full of seventy-five-year-old men, it seems."

Even so, Yoichi says that he does not fear death, as once he might have. It was the death of his sister, four years ago, that made him see things in a different way. Yoichi's voice takes on a new energy when he talks about her.

"She died right here, right here in this house," he says. "She had cancer and was in a great deal of pain. But she was so very brave. All of the family was here to say goodbye. She had so much courage, so much dignity. It really inspired me, that whole experience. After that, I could not possibly be afraid of dying."

Yoichi believes the elderly are treated differently by others. "Drivers are not polite to me. I know I'm a cautious driver, maybe a little slow on the highway."

"IT MADE ME SICK"

There is something that Yoichi has been reluctant to talk about, he says, but it needs to be said. It is the most unpleasant, the most frightening thing that has happened to him in many years.

"I had a break-in here, about a year and a half ago," he says, his face taking on a somber look. "I had been gone between three o'-clock in the afternoon and seven thirty that evening. When I came home, the window of my front door was completely broken in."

Yoichi shakes his head sadly. "It made me sick, just sick. I just knew something was wrong as I drove up the street on the side of my house. I could see the lights on upstairs, and I wouldn't have left those on. I just knew.

"There was glass everywhere, and broken things. All of my things, all of my family's things on the floor, just scattered as if they were rubbish. They took all of the jewelry that had belonged to my sister. They took cameras, too. In the cameras they were not so smart, because I had several cameras, but they only took two of the cheaper ones. Perhaps they did not understand that something old and battered looking could be the most expensive of the bunch."

Yoichi says that that experience has forced him to stay close to home.

"I haven't been out of my house after dark since the break-in, since a year and a half ago," he says. "It is confining, of course. But I am afraid of what might happen if I leave, you see. They might be back; I don't know. And I don't know if the police know, either.

"They said it was probably kids, but that frightens me. Young people so bold and aggressive that they will break into my house to steal my sister's things, that they will tear apart my house? That is what makes me feel scared inside."

"I AM LONELY; I WILL ADMIT THAT"

In large part because of his nervousness about leaving home after dark, but also because he is a shy man, Yoichi says he misses the companionship of other people.

"I am lonely; I will admit that," he says, looking down at his folded hands. "I don't really see other people. Once in a while I drive out to see my sister's grandchildren. They're little enough for me to give piggyback rides to. It's probably as hard on me as shoveling snow, but lots more fun! Anyway, they like that, and I enjoy seeing them. I am not like some old people who don't like children. I don't mind that they're noisy or silly.

"I wish that they lived closer, though. I don't get to see them very often. It's quite a drive. I go in the morning, and sometimes stay for lunch. I need to be back by late afternoon, of course."

Do his grandnieces and grandnephews ever come to visit him in the city? He shakes his head and looks around at his cluttered living room.

"I guess there is not very much for children to do here in this house."

Aside from an occasional drive to see the children, Yoichi says that he doesn't have any other reason to get involved with other people.

"I don't go to many movies. Really, the promotions they have on television look so violent and frightening; maybe I wouldn't even like movies these days. Plus, I don't really know anyone to go to a movie with, or anything," he says. "The last movie I saw was *South Pacific*—in the early 1960s, I think."

He laughs, figuring out how long ago that was. "I guess I was right about not getting out to many movies, eh?

"I don't belong to any clubs or anything, either," he says. "Some old people join activity groups and meet a couple of times each week to play cards, or things like that. But if I ever moved into one of those retirement communities, I would take part in things, that's for sure. I could make friends there.

"Some old people think of those communities as giving up their independence. But no one would force me to do things. I could take it or leave it. But at least there would be people there who would like to talk, or do things. I'd like that. That's probably the answer for me."

Yoichi does not know his neighbors; he says that he doesn't even know their names.

"The people in the big house to the south haven't spoken to me for years," he says. "I once complained about their dog barking all night, and they got mad at me. They don't even look up if we happen to be outside at the same time. And there is a young couple that just moved into the house on the north. The man seems nice, but I haven't been introduced to him."

What about getting out once in a while to do volunteer work? Yoichi shakes his head emphatically.

"I know there are some elderly people who do that sort of thing—go to the library, or to schools to read to children. I could never do that; I'd be afraid. I like children, like I said, but strangers, no. I don't know how other people do that, just walk into a classroom and feel comfortable reading to children. Not for me, not for me."

Yoichi says that he used to be involved in church activities as a young man but that he no longer goes to church.

"There used to be a Japanese church on the northeast side of the city," he says. "They disbanded in the 1960s, though. I'm not sure why. Maybe it was because there was no more interest or because

While healthy enough to maintain his independence, Yoichi fears leaving his home. "I am lonely; I will admit that. . . . I don't really see other people."

the Japanese began feeling more comfortable going to the Caucasian churches with everyone else. I don't know. But I haven't joined another church.

"There is a church in Seattle—the one I belonged to as a child. I still get weekly bulletins from them, and I read them cover to cover. It's something I look forward to getting in the mail each week. Like I said, I read all of it, even though I don't know any of the people they mention. And I send a donation each Christmas."

"I HAVE PLENTY TO DO"

Yoichi insists that although he does lead a very solitary life, he is not unhappy.

Yoichi spends his days slowly going through his belongings in an effort to sell his house. "At this rate, I'll be in my nineties before the house is ready to go."

"My main ambition is to sell this house," he says. "I'm trying very hard to get the house cleaned out. I might move back to Seattle. That would be my first choice right now. Since I grew up there, it might be fun to go back now, I think.

"If I don't go to Seattle, I think I'll just get a smaller place here in this area. Like I said before, an apartment in an old people's community would be nice. Plus, I wouldn't have to worry about break-ins. I guess that's the main thing."

Yoichi says that it is a lot of work getting the house ready to sell. He points out some of the problems—the worn spot in the kitchen linoleum and the dangerous-looking wiring.

"There are not enough outlets in this old house," he says. "Someone buying this place will have a lot to fix up. But it's a nice house, and I have decided not to fix all the troubles. It would be great for young people with lots of energy, with the skill to fix things themselves. I'd ask a lower price, but I'd sell it faster."

It is a little sad going through all of his family's belongings, he says. It is difficult to know what might be important or useful later on. "Sometimes a day will go by, and I won't have accomplished anything except maybe throw away a newspaper from many years ago," he says. "I can't just pick up a stack and throw it away, because someone must have saved the papers for some reason. I have to look through them carefully, to see what might have been the reason. It takes lots of time, and I'm not getting much done.

"At this rate," he laughs, "I'll be in my nineties before the house is ready to go."

Epilogue

In the time since they were first interviewed for this book, the four people whose stories make up *The Other America: The Elderly* have had changes in their lives which readers would no doubt find interesting.

Lois has been busy, as always. She spent most of the winter living in Arizona, and this past summer enjoyed visiting Alaska for three weeks. She continues to enjoy good health.

Clarence, whose health seemed in the winter of 1995 to be deteriorating rapidly, is now feeling much better. "I'm healthier than I've been in a year," he says. He is not as homebound as he was before, and enjoys occasional trips to church on Sundays. "It sure makes a difference when you feel good," he says in his booming bass.

Martha is also feeling better. The sickness which made her legs numb and tingly, and which prevented her from doing much walking, seems to be going away. She continues to be active in the workings of the care facility in which she lives, taking photographs at social get-togethers and sharing them with others. "The workers finally finished the courtyard," she says, "and we had a nice dedication ceremony. There's a new flagpole, and a weather vane, too." She has been reading and writing lots of letters to friends.

Yoichi has been bothered lately by arthritis in his right hip. Doctors have advised him that hip replacement would be the best thing for him, but he is worried about being away from his house for any length of time. Since the break-in, he says, he just hasn't felt comfortable about leaving. He is looking forward to the visit of his sister from Texas. She comes up about once a year, and he enjoys catching up on all her news.

Ways You Can Get Involved

THERE ARE MANY WAYS TO BECOME INVOLVED IN THE LIVES OF ELDERLY PEOPLE

■ Choose aging as a topic for a social studies or science report. Interview several elderly people for your report.

■ Many nursing homes will accept and train volunteers. Ask about how to become involved for an hour or two each week.

■ Adopt an honorary grandmother or grandfather. Befriend an elderly person in your neighborhood. Rake leaves, shovel snow, or simply spend a few minutes each day talking and listening to him or her.

■ Write to the following organizations that publish information on the topic of elderly people:

American Association of Retired Persons (AARP)
601 E St. NW
Washington, DC 20049
This organization works to inform the elderly about issues and candidates and mobilize them into an effective voting force.

Elderhostel
75 Federal St.
Third Floor
Boston, MA 02110
Elderhostel promotes leisure, travel, and learning programs for the elderly in more than forty-seven countries around the world. Elderhostel students range in age from sixty to ninety-three.

Gray Panthers
2025 Pennsylvania Ave. NW, Suite 821
Washington, DC 20006
This organization is founded on the idea that both old and young have many things to contribute to life in America. The Gray Panthers fight is against ageism, discrimination against the elderly.

For Further Reading

Andrew W. Achenbaum, *Old Age in the New Land: The American Aging Experience Since 1790*. Baltimore: Johns Hopkins University Press, 1978. An interesting book, detailing the differences in how Americans have treated the elderly throughout history.

Ken Dychtwald and Joe Flower, *Age Wave: The Challenges and Opportunities of an Aging America*. Los Angeles: Jeremy P. Tarcher, 1989. Centers on the future of America as baby boomers grow old.

Edward Edelson, *Aging*. New York: Chelsea House, 1991. Good bibliography and helpful index. Discusses the various issues of elderly people today, including an interesting discussion of the ways elderly people differ in mental and physical capacities from younger people.

John Langone, *Growing Older: What Young People Should Know About Aging*. Boston: Little, Brown, 1991. Highly readable book that examines the misconceptions and half-truths that younger people have about old people.

Alvin Silverstein and Glenn Silverstein, *Aging*. New York: Franklin Watts, 1979. Helpful book for young readers, detailing various aspects of the aging process and focusing on the changing attitudes American society has toward its elderly citizens.

Index

ABOUT THE AUTHOR

Gail B. Stewart is the author of more than eighty books for children and young adults. She lives in Minneapolis, Minnesota, with her husband Carl and their sons Ted, Eliot, and Flynn. When she is not writing, she spends her time reading, walking, and watching her sons play soccer.

Although she has enjoyed working on each of her books, she says that *The Other America* series has been especially gratifying. "So many of my past books have involved extensive research," she says, "but most of it has been library work—journals, magazines, books. But for these books, the main research has been very human. Spending the day with a little girl who has AIDS, or having lunch in a soup kitchen with a homeless man—these kinds of things give you insight that a library alone just can't match."

Stewart hopes that readers of this series will experience some of the same insights—perhaps even being motivated to use some of the suggestions at the end of each book to become involved with someone of the Other America.

ABOUT THE PHOTOGRAPHER

Mark Ahlstrom has worked in publishing for over twenty years, producing over two hundred books for young adults.